THE WILDERNESS OF THE SOUTHWEST

THE WILDERNESS OF THE SOUTHWEST

*CHARLES SHELDON'S QUEST FOR DESERT BIGHORN SHEEP
AND ADVENTURES WITH THE HAVASUPAI AND SERI INDIANS*

EDITED BY NEIL B. CARMONY
AND DAVID E. BROWN

UNIVERSITY OF UTAH PRESS
SALT LAKE CITY

Library of Congress Cataloging-in-Publication Data

Sheldon, Charles, 1867–1928.
    The wilderness of the Southwest : Charles Sheldon's quest for
desert bighorn sheep and adventures with the Havasupai and
Seri Indians / edited by Neil B. Carmony and David E. Brown.
        p.   cm.
    Includes bibliographical references and index.
    Journals previously published in an edited version as: The
Wilderness of desert bighorns & Seri Indians. 1979.
    ISBN 0-87480-417-5
    1. Bighorn sheep hunting—Arizona. 2. Bighorn sheep hunt-
ing—Mexico—Sonora (State) 3. Seri Indian—Social life and cus-
toms. 4. Sheldon, Charles, 1867–1928—Diaries. 5. Hunters—
Diaries.
I. Carmony, Neil B. II. Brown, David E. (David Earl), 1938– .
III. Sheldon, Charles, 1867–1928. Wilderness of desert bighorns
& Seri Indians. IV. Title.
SK305.B45S535   1993
799.2'77358—dc20   93-4421

For Eleanor Sheldon Lunde

Contents

MAPS

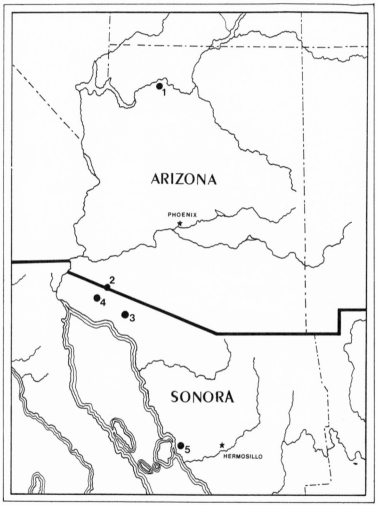

Arizona and northern Sonora, Mexico, with Charles Sheldon's Southwest hunting locales. 1. Grand Canyon (1912). 2. Tinajas Altas and vicinity (1913). 3. Sierra Pinacate (1915). 4. Sierra del Rosario (1916). 5. Sierra Seri and Tiburón Island (1921–1922).

Foreword

Each night during his North American big-game collecting expeditions, no matter how tired he was, Charles Sheldon (1867–1928) faithfully recorded the day's events in his journal. These journals were the basis for two books on his northern adventures that were published during his lifetime: *The Wilderness of the Upper Yukon* (1911) and *The Wilderness of the North Pacific Coast Islands* (1912). Both were published by Charles Scribner's Sons in New York. A third volume, *The Wilderness of Denali*, was in manuscript form when Sheldon died and was published posthumously by Scribner's in 1930. In the introduction to what he believed to be Sheldon's final work, the editor, Sheldon's friend and colleague Dr. C. Hart Merriam, wrote: "Thus *The Wilderness of Denali* completes the account of his hunting expeditions in the Far North. . . . But nowhere except in his precious journals may be found accounts of his sheep hunts in the Grand and Havasu Canyons of Arizona and those on the desert mountains of Sonora, nor of his visit and deer hunt with the Sére Indians of Tiburon Island in the Gulf of California."

Now, more than sixty years later, Charles Sheldon's desert adventures are available for all to read. Carefully preserved by his family, his Southwest journals were taken by his son, Dr. William Sheldon, to Dr. Lyle K. Sowls, Cooperative Wildlife Research Unit Leader at the University of Arizona, in 1978. Dr. Sowls contacted the editors of this volume, who, through the efforts of Arizona Game and Fish Department Game Branch Supervisor Paul M. Webb, engaged the interest of the Arizona Desert Bighorn Sheep Society in publishing the journals. The result was a private printing in 1979 of a rather heavily edited version of the journals entitled *The Wilderness of Desert Bighorns and Seri Indians.* Limited to one thousand copies, this edition is now out of print.

In 1980, William Sheldon donated his father's original Southwest journals and photographs to the Special Collections Department of the University of Arizona Library at Tucson. Wanting to make Charles Sheldon's fascinating adventures available to a wider reading public, the senior editor prepared a new transcription of the diaries, taking care to preserve Sheldon's campfire writing style. It is this transcription, together with a biographical profile of this truly remarkable man, explanatory headnotes for each of his five expeditions, and a short epilogue summarizing Sheldon's Southwest legacy and the present status of the lands that he hunted, that we present here through the auspices of the University of Utah Press.

Neil B. Carmony
David E. Brown

Introduction

CHARLES SHELDON
HUNTER, NATURALIST, CONSERVATIONIST

Rutland, Vermont, could not have a more attractive setting. Nestled in Otter Creek Valley in the Green Mountains, the town is surrounded by forests that are laced with trout streams and dotted with lakes. Lush and verdant in summer, a riot of colors in fall, a sparkling wonderland in winter, south-central Vermont was, and is, an ideal place for a boy to grow up. Here, Charles Alexander Sheldon, the first child of John and Carolyn Sheldon, was born on October 17, 1867. He would eventually have three sisters and three brothers.

The Sheldons were well-to-do. The source of the family's income was the Sheldon and Sons Marble Company, founded in 1850 by Charles Sheldon's grandfather and namesake, Charles M. A. Sheldon (1813–1889). Marble quarrying became a viable enterprise when the Rutland and Burlington Railroad was completed through Otter Creek Valley in 1849, and the industry flourished. Rutland marble soon became famous throughout the Northeast, for both beauty and durability.

John A. Sheldon (1839–1910) served with distinction in the First and Tenth regiments of the Vermont Volunteers during the Civil War. After returning home to Rutland, he married Carolyn Eastman and joined the marble firm owned by his father. He was active in local politics and was elected to the town council and served a term in the state legislature. In the early 1880s, John assumed the management of the family business. His three younger brothers also worked for the firm, which now had about 140 employees. The largest marble producer in Rutland County, however, was the Vermont Marble Company. It accounted for nearly half of the county's marble, Sheldon and Sons was next in size, and there were several smaller firms.

John Sheldon built a large, elegant home in Rutland, Vermont's second largest city, but it was the surrounding country-side that most interested young Charles. Summers were spent in the woods, hunting rabbits and squirrels and fishing for brook trout and walleyes. In the fall, the quarry was waterfowl and ruffed grouse. He loved to practice woodcraft and became an expert at handling a canoe and wielding an ax. His talent with a fly rod was admired by men much older than he, as was his skill at wingshooting. As a boy, Charles Sheldon greatly admired his paternal grandfather and tried to model himself after him. A kindly man, his grandfather also had a forceful personality and was much respected in Rutland. He truly lived by the Victorian virtues of self-discipline, personal honesty, and devotion to duty.

John and Carolyn Sheldon wanted the best possible education for their oldest son, and they could afford it. In 1882, Charles Sheldon was enrolled at Phillips Academy, a posh prep school in Andover, Massachusetts. Four years later he was admitted to Yale College, one of the training grounds for the sons of America's social and political elite. A classmate and life-long friend, Leonard C. Sanford, in a 1929 memoir describing Sheldon's days at New Haven, recalled that Sheldon had a liberal allowance and was a "free spender." He liked to socialize and was "well-liked and popular." Muscular and athletic, Sheldon was a member of the Yale rowing team. When he entered college as a member of the class of 1890, he was described as an adequate student, although he was casual about his studies. He took courses in science and mathematics, but he was more interested in literature and poetry and became a member of the Elizabethan Club, a literary discussion group.

During his freshman year, an incident occurred that demonstrated Charles Sheldon's rugged determination. He had recently taken up the flute and was proud of the expensive instrument that he owned. One afternoon he noticed that the flute was missing. A frantic search failed to find it. Earlier in the day a salesman from New York had been seen about the students' quarters peddling cigars. He had entered Sheldon's room but quickly left, having failed to make a sale. Sheldon and his classmates concluded the cigar salesman had stolen the prized flute.

Sheldon immediately left the campus and caught a train for New York, about 80 miles away. The next day he contacted the police and was advised to check certain pawn shops that dealt in high-quality musical instruments—he might find his flute in one of them. Sheldon began going from shop to shop, but with no luck. Then, as he was leaving one of the pawn shops, he saw the cigar salesman coming down the street toward him. In the man's pocket was Sheldon's missing flute. The man did not recognize Sheldon as they passed, and Sheldon jumped the thief from behind and wrestled him to the sidewalk. A crowd gathered, and a policeman showed up. After all was said and done, Sheldon was on the train back to New Haven with his flute and the cigar peddler was cooling his heels in jail. Sheldon described the affair in a letter to his father, which was printed in the Rutland newspaper. The article concluded with the observation that "Even detectives are born in Rutland."

The latter part of the 1880s saw the Sheldon family business suffer financial disaster. Competition with the larger Vermont Marble Company was fierce, and Sheldon and Sons had gradually become overwhelmed with debt. By the end of his sophomore year at Yale, Charles Sheldon's liberal allowance had been reduced to a pittance. Although he was able to remain in school, his attitude underwent a profound change. No longer a free-spending, happy-go-lucky college boy, he became a serious student concerned about his future. As his father's company slid into bankruptcy, young Sheldon knew that he would have to make his own way in the world without the financial backing of his family. Indeed, as the eldest son, much of the burden of supporting the family, and educating his brothers and sisters, would fall on him. In 1891, the few remaining assets of Sheldon and Sons Marble Company were sold to the Vermont Marble Company—the year after Charles received his bachelor of arts degree from Yale.

During the late summer of 1890, Charles Sheldon accompanied classmate Leonard Sanford on an extended waterfowl hunt in the Magdalen Islands in the Gulf of St. Lawrence. On their return, Sanford went off to medical school and Sheldon accepted a job with the Lake Shore and Michigan Southern Railway Company. Another classmate, A. B. Newell, helped him land this job as a junior management official—Newell's father was president of the company. As a young supervisor, Sheldon was stationed first at Chicago, then Toledo, then Elkhart, Indiana. While he was serving in Toledo, a trainmen's strike threatened to disrupt the railroad's operations. Charles Sheldon was credited with being the one chiefly responsible for settling the strike to the satisfaction of both labor and management. His success as a supervisor was largely due to the fact that he genuinely liked people, regardless of their backgrounds. Throughout his life he would treat backwoodsmen, Mexican *vaqueros*, Indians, and all the other people he met, with respect, knowing that they each possessed valuable skills and knowledge.

In 1894, Charles Sheldon accepted a position as general manager and treasurer of the Consolidated Car Heating Company in Albany, New York. The company manufactured equipment for railroad cars, and it prospered under Sheldon's leadership. While in Albany, Sheldon became acquainted with Dean Sage, a lumber tycoon who controlled vast tracts of timberland in both the United States and Canada. Although Sage's main offices were in New York City, he had a large lumber yard in Albany and maintained a home there. This was the age of American industrial giants, and men like Sage were awash in money. He had become interested in investing in railroads and mines in Chihuahua, Mexico, as the subsidies and other inducements offered by the Díaz government were most attractive. In 1898, Sage recruited Charles Sheldon to oversee the Chihuahuan enterprises that he and a group of American capitalists were intent on bankrolling. One of the investors was Colonel Oliver H. Payne, one of the richest men in America. Payne's industrial empire included large holdings in steel mills, railroads, oil, and mines. It was reported that his share of the Standard Oil Company was second only to John D. Rockefeller's. Payne had attended both Phillips Academy and Yale College and had great confidence in Sheldon because of their similar educational backgrounds. His confidence in the young manager proved to be well placed.

Charles Sheldon was not eager to leave his friends and family in the Northeast to live and work in a foreign country. His career in Albany was going well and he was content with his role in life. But he was young (thirty-one), a bachelor, and, in simple terms, Sage and Payne made him an offer he could not refuse. His salary would be generous, and with bonuses and profit-sharing arrangements, he could look forward to returning to the United States in a few years as a wealthy man. Late in 1898, Sheldon resigned from the Consolidated Car Heating Company and accepted a position as general manager of the Chihuahua and Pacific Railway Company and the Chihuahua and Pacific Exploration Company.

The Chihuahuan enterprises were joint ventures with Mexican investors. The Mexican interests were principally represented by Enrique C. Creel, a banker and politician who was one of the great deal-makers in Porfirio Díaz's Mexico. Creel was ideally suited for promoting business deals with American capitalists. He was the son of Reuben W. Creel, American consul at Chihuahua City during the 1850s and 1860s, and Paz Cuilty, a member of an influential Mexican family. Although a Mexican citizen, Enrique Creel spoke fluent English and, through his father, had important American contacts. But his real power derived from his being the favorite son-in-law of Don Luis Terrazas, one of the wealthiest men in Mexico and one of the world's largest landowners. Don Luis' *haciendas* encompassed between six and seven million acres of Chihuahua's choicest grazing lands, an area larger than Sheldon's home state of Vermont. Through his sons and sons-in-law, Terrazas controlled another eight million acres. By comparison, the fabled King Ranch in Texas in its heyday included only about one and a quarter million acres. But the Terrazas empire included much more than land, cattle, and sheep. The Terrazas family owned flour mills, textile mills, breweries, mines, banks, and urban real estate. Not much took place in Chihuahua in the 1890s without the involvement of a Terrazas. Enrique Creel had primary responsibility for managing the vast Terrazas holdings.

As early as the 1870s, railroad promoters had observed that
the shortest route from the American Midwest to the Pacific
Ocean was not west to California, but southwest across Texas,
Chihuahua, and the Sierra Madre to the west coast of Mexico.
St. Louis was 350 miles closer to the deepwater port of
Topolobampo, Sinaloa, than to San Francisco. Shortly after the
Mexican Central Railroad connected Chihuahua City with El
Paso in 1884, a group of investors received a concession from the
Díaz government to build a rail line from Chihuahua City to the
Pacific. No construction was undertaken, however, and in 1897
the concession was acquired by Enrique Creel. The aggressive
Creel immediately began assembling a consortium of American
capitalists to participate in the project, including Dean Sage and
Colonel Payne.

Charles Sheldon arrived in Chihuahua City in December
1898. His first priority was to establish a working relationship
with his Mexican counterparts, then get construction under
way. Although Creel's ultimate goal was reaching the west coast
of Mexico, the Americans were primarily concerned with the
100-mile stretch from Chihuahua City to the village of Miñaca
in the Sierra Madre foothills. A railroad line to Miñaca would
open up the Sierra's rich ranching, lumbering, and mining
resources to exploitation, and several American companies had
obtained concessions in the region. Construction went
smoothly, and the railway to Miñaca was completed in the summer of 1900.

Shortly after arriving in Chihuahua, Sheldon wrote a letter
to a Mrs. Hamilin in Boston describing his situation in Mexico:

> I have been here three months, occupied in perpetual work —
> day and night — and the time seems long before a system can
> be made so the enjoyment of a little leisure time will come.
> The work is a large undertaking and together with some min-
> ing enterprises they have put in my charge, my time and
> thoughts have been filled. I live pleasantly, very pleasantly, in
> a delightful little Mexican house about a mile from Chihua-
> hua City. It is in the rear of 20 acres and has a large cultivated
> tropical garden. There are many flowering trees, hosts of roses

and flowers, an open-air bath, and the most beautiful scenery around. There is a servant's house and a large corral for my horse when I have time to use one. I have imported furniture, my books, and a Japanese servant imported from N.Y. . . . . I am absolutely alone and can find no congenial companions here. My love for nature and all that it brings, the outdoor life, and my books will, in time, be indulged. . . . I have given up a good deal and my present life is a strange and hard contrast to that delightful four years in Albany. But it is my disposition to make the best of anything, so I am busy and contented and happy. Every day I am glad I am here and see my opportunities growing. . . . I often wonder what sort of a product these varied experiences, adaptation to new people and conditions, and a general broadening will make of me. Here, under these sunny skies, I must while away a few years. . . . Some of the lands here are beautiful. My railroad will bring me in contact with a wide range of country and offer many chances for enjoying a little recreation when I get time. I am beginning to speak Spanish after some hard work. It is necessary down here.

Sheldon had always loved to hunt, and Chihuahua offered almost unlimited opportunities to indulge in this sport. In New England his hunting had been restricted to small game. In Chihuahua he found a big-game hunter's paradise, and Sheldon availed himself of every chance to go afield. The grasslands that make the state a cattleman's heaven were the home of numerous pronghorn; the rough desert ranges to the north provided habitat for bighorn sheep; the desert foothills contained mule deer; the Sierra Madre proper was the domain of white-tailed deer, mountain lions, wolves, wild turkeys, black bears, and the monarch of the mountains, the grizzly.

On his hunting trips, Sheldon was usually accompanied by the cowboys who worked on the huge *ranchos* owned by the oligarchs. In a remembrance of his days afield in Chihuahua, Sheldon described his *compadres*:

Mexican vaqueros, employed for general assistance, were my companions, or, more precisely, good well-tested friends.

They always maintained the most friendly cheerfulness and genuine interest in the success of my trips. No amount of work ever diminished their happy spirits; more than anything else they enjoyed being out in camp and all the vicissitudes of life in the wilderness.

Two big-game animals especially fascinated Sheldon—grizzlies and mountain sheep. He would spend much of the next two decades in search of these animals throughout North America. Pursuing these species required tramping among the magnificent wilderness mountains, an activity he found exhilarating. Grizzlies were creatures of the remotest *barrancas*; bighorn sheep inhabited the most rugged *sierras*. Sheldon loved hunting these animals because they took him into the mountains, and he was becoming as much a mountaineer as a hunter. Although of only average size (5 feet 10 inches in height and weighing about 170 pounds), he possessed remarkable strength and endurance. Those who hunted with him never failed to be impressed by his ability to pack heavy loads for long distances through rough terrain. Only the most rugged companions could keep up with him when hiking among Sheldon's cherished mountain peaks.

In September 1901, Vice President Theodore Roosevelt became president of the United States after the assassination of William McKinley. That fall, Dean Sage asked Sheldon if he could arrange a Mexican bear hunt for the new president. Sheldon had never met Roosevelt, but he greatly admired him, and gladly accepted the assignment. Immediately he contacted Johnny Bell, manager of the million-acre Babicora Ranch northwest of Chihuahua City. The American-owned Babicora contained some of the best grizzly and black bear habitat in Mexico, and Sheldon was sure the president would be thrilled with the hunting there. After all the plans were made, Roosevelt found out that the ranch was owned by Phoebe Hearst, widow of Senator George Hearst and mother of newspaperman William Randolph Hearst. The president promptly canceled the hunt. The Hearst newspapers had supported William Jennings Bryan for president in 1900, and had viciously attacked the McKinley-Roosevelt ticket. Teddy was still hot about it.

Not wanting his elaborate hunting arrangements to go for naught, Sheldon invited his friend Leonard Sanford to come to Chihuahua and hunt with him. Sanford accepted. After spending several days in Chihuahua City, the two men took the train to Miñaca, where they were met by Johnny Bell and taken into the mountains by wagon. They had a fabulous hunt. The men bagged two grizzlies, a black bear, and several white-tailed deer and turkeys. Leaving the Babicora Ranch, the hunters went several miles to the east to a desert mountain range to hunt bighorn sheep. Both got rams, but the biggest one seen, a grand old ram, gave them the slip. "The most extraordinary hunting trip I ever went on," wrote Sanford.

Sheldon still loved wingshooting, and he took Sanford to a slough on one of Terrazas' ranches. Here they shot fifteen to twenty ducks apiece and could have killed many more. Most of the birds were given to the people living at the ranch. Although they did not have time to visit Sheldon's favorite waterfowl marsh, Sheldon described it to Sanford in detail. Laguna de Bustillos was (and is) a large, marshy lake about 40 miles west of Chihuahua City. It was on land owned by the Zuloaga family, related by marriage to Luis Terrazas. During the winter months the lake was covered with ducks and geese, and when time permitted, Sheldon would go out to the ranch and spend the night. The next morning he would put out decoys and enjoy waterfowl shooting that he believed to be unequaled anywhere in North America.

One last anecdote provided by Sanford must be mentioned. Soon after arriving in Chihuahua City, Sheldon inquired about hiring someone to guide him into the high country west of town. He was advised to see a young butcher who had spent several years roaming the sierras and who had only recently settled in the city. The man agreed to guide Sheldon, and they had a most enjoyable trip. It was not until later, after the butcher had left town, that Sheldon learned that his guide, Francisco "Pancho" Villa, was an outlaw and that he had returned to the mountains to resume his career as a bandit and cattle rustler.

The railroad to Miñaca having been successfully completed, Sheldon could devote more of his energies to the Pacific Exploration Company, which was also showing signs of promise. Following the advice of a shrewd mining engineer named Phillips, the company, under Sheldon's direction, acquired a silver and lead mine in the Santa Eulalia mining district about 15 miles southeast of Chihuahua City. Silver had been mined in the district since the 1700s, but an infusion of foreign capital and mining expertise was now pushing production to unprecedented levels. The mine, the El Potosí, quickly became the richest silver producer in Chihuahua. Sheldon was awarded a $1/36$ interest in the mine in recognition of his services to the company. This marked a turning point in Sheldon's career—earnings from the El Potosí would make him financially independent for the rest of his life.

In the fall of 1902, Sheldon said good-bye to Enrique Creel, Luis Terrazas, Carlos Zuloaga, and his other Mexican business associates, along with the vaqueros with whom he had spent so many glorious days, and returned to the United States. Settling in New York, he dabbled for a brief time in the cement business, then retired from active business affairs in 1903. He was thirty-five years old.

Sheldon was aware that the U.S. Biological Survey was conducting an intensive biological inventory throughout Mexico, and this project intrigued him. Late in 1903 he went to Washington, D.C., to visit the Biological Survey office to compare notes with the professional naturalists. There he met Dr. C. Hart Merriam, chief of the bureau, and Edward W. Nelson, senior field naturalist in charge of the Mexican survey. The three men hit it off immediately, and Sheldon and Nelson became close friends.

Under Merriam's far-seeing leadership, the Biological Survey was actively collecting museum specimens of plants and animals throughout North America. Merriam realized that America's wildlife was a part of a continentwide biota, and to understand the larger biological system, he had sent collectors to Canada and Mexico as well as U.S. territory. Government bureaus and museums had small staffs in those days, and they were heavily dependent on private citizens for their collections. Professional collectors commonly sold specimens to institutions, and amateurs frequently donated others. It was still a time when un-trained but hardy adventurers could make genuine contribu-tions by sampling the biota of little-known corners of the globe. Such an activity greatly appealed to Sheldon, and he was quickly recruited by Merriam and Nelson as an unpaid zoologi-cal collector.

Edward Nelson had spent four years in the 1870s in Alaska as a weather observer for the U.S. Army Signal Corps. While in Alaska, Nelson, then in his twenties, had spent much of his time collecting specimens and Eskimo artifacts for the U.S. National Museum. In his collection were a series of white sheep that he had acquired from local hunters—the first specimens of these animals known to science. Nelson published a description of these sheep in 1884, naming them *Ovis montana dalli* in honor of William Dall, an early Alaska explorer. The sheep of the region were still poorly known, however, and the range of Dall sheep had yet to be delineated. Sheldon, who was intensely interested in wild sheep, jumped at the suggestion that he hunt and observe the sheep of the Far North. An expedition to Yukon Territory was quickly planned.

In July 1904, Sheldon arrived in the Yukon in the company of Dr. Wilfred Osgood of the Biological Survey and wildlife artist and fellow volunteer Carl Rungius. For the next three months the three men hunted and collected, Sheldon concen-trating on sheep, Rungius on moose, caribou, and bears, and Osgood trapping small mammals and shooting birds. While in the wilderness, the party ran into the famous British hunter-explorer Frederick Selous, who was after caribou and moose. Sheldon had read Selous' books detailing his exploits in South Africa and thought highly of the old ivory hunter and collector for the British Museum. Selous teamed up with the Americans and hunted and camped with them for the remaining six weeks of the summer. Although the fifty-three-year-old Selous was six-teen years older than Sheldon, the two hunters struck up a life-long friendship.

After a successful collecting season, the hunters left the Yukon as the October snows began to fall. Before returning to New York, Sheldon spent a month hunting wapiti on Vancouver Island. Hampered by heavy fogs and rain, he managed to bag only one female for a specimen.

Back in New York, Sheldon was elected to membership in the prestigious Boone and Crockett Club, an organization of sportsmen-conservationists founded in 1887 by Theodore Roosevelt and George Bird Grinnell among others. Sheldon had been sponsored for membership by Edward Nelson. The club was limited to one hundred regular members, whose primary purpose was "to work for the preservation of the large game of this country." The Boone and Crockett Club was thus to big-game animals what the Audubon Society was to birds. Indeed, Grinnell had also helped found the first Audubon Society in 1886. Naturalist, author, ethnologist, and publisher of *Forest and Stream* magazine, Grinnell would become Sheldon's mentor as he developed into a conservation activist.

The month of May 1905 was spent among the huge brown bears of Montague Island off the coast of Alaska. These amazing bears, a subspecies of grizzly, simply fascinated Sheldon with their size and agility. They were abundant on the island, and he had no trouble getting the specimens he needed. Returning to the mainland, he made his way into the interior of the Yukon and continued his inventory of the wild sheep of the region. This time he hired a local packer to care for the horses and keep camp, but he hunted the precipitous mountains alone. He was never happier than when he was on a solitary climb on a wilderness peak. Sheldon described the equipment he used on his northern expeditions in the introduction of his book *The Wilderness of the Upper Yukon*:

> In the way of field equipment, I had an open canvas shelter instead of a tent. . . . No one who loves camp life can prefer a tent to a shelter, except in winter. The log fire which is always made before the shelter reflects warmth directly inside, so that one can sit at ease and in enjoyment in all but the coldest weather. . . . For sleeping I had a coon-skin robe, eight feet square. It weighed fourteen pounds. It keeps me warm enough even in winter weather. A lynx-skin robe is better and warmer, but more expensive. A caribou- or reindeer-skin robe

is the best of all. Equally warm, it is very much lighter than the others. The wolf-skin robe is more commonly used by trappers and prospectors, but is heavier. . . . Heavy woolen socks and moccasins (leather, or preferably moosehide when to be had in sufficient quantity) provide the footgear necessary for summer. . . . I never wore a coat, but instead carried a parkay, or seamless cloak, made of the skins of ground squirrels. . . . A pair of Zeiss prism field-glasses, eight or ten power, an Eastman Kodak for films $3\frac{1}{4}$ x $4\frac{1}{4}$ were always carried on my belt. . . . One of the most important things was my Alpine rucksack which had been made in Germany. . . . In it were the parkay and any extra things needed. Sixty pounds of meat could be packed into it, or a whole bear skin, or the head and skin of a ram. One small canvas bag would hold all my equipment for a season, except the small mouse traps and the steel traps. A common pocket knife of good steel for skinning, a compass, a barometer and a steel tape were always in my pockets. Usually I bought the provisions commonly used by all prospectors and trappers of the country – flour, rice, sugar, dried fruit, butter in tins, tea, bacon and salt. . . . Skins were cured with salt. . . . I always had a .22 rifle to use for shooting grouse and small animals.

For hunting sheep and other big-game animals, Sheldon used a 6.5 x 54R rifle built by Jeffery of England using an 1895 Dutch Mannlicher bolt action. This 6.5 mm (.256 caliber) rifle was the only firearm he ever used for big game. Perhaps because of his "go light" ethic, he never took a spare rifle should the Jeffery give him trouble. This lack of a spare would cause him grief on more than one occasion. On his southwestern expeditions, his equipment was much the same except that he substituted a canvas tarp for the lean-to shelter, always carried a canteen, and left his squirrel-skin "parkay" at home.

Sheldon spent four months among the Yukon's mountains, searching for sheep and making notes on their habits. He collected a useful series of specimens and determined the ranges of the sheep's various color phases. His nearly two years of effort transformed him from an amateur naturalist into the foremost

expert on the mountain sheep of this enormous Canadian territory. But his work in the North was not over. From July to October 1906, he hunted sheep and grizzlies at the base of the highest
mountain on the continent, Mount McKinley. The grandeur of
the scenery, the total wildness, and the wildlife in pristine abundance all combined to overwhelm Sheldon like no place he had
ever seen or imagined. Here he could see hundreds of Dall sheep
in a single day. Grizzlies, moose, and caribou, too, were to be
found in incredible numbers. The enormity of the landscape
swallowed up a mere man, and Sheldon knew that he must
return to this majestic place.

On his way back to the States, Sheldon spent a month
searching for caribou on Graham Island, the largest of the
Queen Charlotte group of islands off the coast of British Columbia. The isolated population of caribou on this wooded island
was small, however, and he was unable to locate any animals.
Only a few old droppings showed that caribou were yet present.
As the rains poured down, Sheldon had to admit defeat—one of
the few times he failed to collect any specimens of the animals he
sought. The Graham Island caribou are now extinct.

Although Sheldon joined many conservation organizations,
he devoted most of his conservation energy to the programs of
the then influential Boone and Crockett Club. On his return to
New York, Sheldon was elected to the club's policy-making
body, the executive committee. His work with the club soon
brought Sheldon to the attention of its founder, now president
of the United States. It was only natural that Roosevelt and
Sheldon should become good friends. Besides their mutual interests in hunting, natural history, and conservation, both of them
liked outdoor writing and were avid book collectors. Sheldon
became a frequent visitor at the White House and Sagamore
Hill, Roosevelt's home on Long Island.

Sheldon returned to Alaska and Mount McKinley in the
summer of 1907. With the help of Harry Karstens, a local guide
who had worked for him the previous year, Sheldon built a log
cabin in the shadow of Denali, "the high one," as Mount
McKinley was called by the Indians. His plan was to spend the
winter at the base of the mountain and observe sheep and other

Charles Sheldon feeds a gray jay near his cabin in Alaska. #76–42–4, William Sheldon Collection, Alaska and Polar Regions Department, University of Alaska, Fairbanks.

animals through an entire annual cycle. Karstens would keep him supplied by packhorse or dogsled as conditions required.

Karstens had come to Alaska during the gold rush of 1897 at the age of eighteen. Although he failed to find gold, he stayed on, working at a number of frontier occupations. Sheldon liked and respected Karstens, calling him "one of the best dog drivers in the North." During the coming winter, Sheldon would depend on Karstens for his very survival. His faith was not misplaced; the Alaskan "sourdough" was both capable and reliable.

Sheldon spent the next several months collecting specimens, making weather observations, and carefully recording the activities of sheep and other wildlife. Many days and nights were spent away from his cabin, camping in a small tent, to be near the animals he was studying. For weeks on end he endured temperatures that never rose above freezing. Yet, he left Denali in June 1908 with reluctance. "No words," he wrote, "can describe my sorrow and regret as I led the horse out of the woods from the cabin to the bar and started down the river. I was leaving

forever this region in which I had lived and hunted with a feeling of complete possession." The year Charles Sheldon spent
beneath the towering Denali still ranks as one of the greatest
adventures undertaken in the service of natural science.

Sheldon returned home to find Mount McKinley much in
the news. Dr. Frederick Cook had recently published an article
in *Harper's Magazine* announcing that he and another man had
been the first to ascend to the summit of the 20,300-foot mountain in September 1906. Although Cook had genuine creden-
tials as an explorer, some mountaineers were dubious of his
claim. Nonetheless, Cook's accomplishment was accepted by
several geographical and exploration societies, and Sheldon had
no reason to doubt him. He therefore agreed to contribute a
chapter on the Indians of Alaska to Cook's forthcoming book,
To the Top of the Continent. Dr. Wilfred Osgood also agreed to
write a description of the mammals Sheldon had collected in the
vicinity of Mount McKinley for the same book.

Then Cook dropped an even larger bombshell. On September 1, 1909, Cook announced that he had reached the
North Pole on April 21, 1908. Five days later, on September 6,
Commodore Robert Peary cabled the news to the world that he
had reached the North Pole on April 6, 1909. A protracted and
bitter debate ensued about who had been the first man to stand
at the North Pole, as Peary hotly disputed Cook's claim.
Although many expert explorers backed Cook at first, most of
them, after examining all of the evidence produced, threw their
support to Peary. Suspected of being a fraud, Cook and his
earlier claim to having climbed Mount McKinley now came
under fire. Again, a careful review of the evidence disclosed that
Cook had faked photographs and other data. Cook's account
was shown conclusively to be bogus. Sheldon had been deceived
by Cook and was not pleased, but it was too late to retrieve his
contributions to Cook's book, which had been published in
1908. In the future he would view claims made by other explorers with great caution. Mount McKinley was finally climbed in
1913 by a party of four that included Harry Karstens. If his
friend Karstens was involved, Sheldon knew that this time the
claim was genuine.

While Charles Sheldon was tramping the slopes of Mount McKinley, a plan to protect the area and its wildlife for future generations emerged in his mind. What better place for a grand national park than the continent's highest mountain? At the annual meeting of the Boone and Crockett Club in January 1909, Sheldon presented his Denali National Park plan, complete with lantern slides showing the magnificent landscapes, and maps with suggested boundaries. The proposal was well received but no action was taken. The club was then deeply immersed in an effort to create Glacier National Park, a pet project of George Bird Grinnell. Grinnell pointed out that the threats to the lands within the proposed park in Montana were much more immediate than those facing Denali. In fact it took nineteen years of dogged work by Grinnell before the great conservationist's beloved Glacier National Park was created by Congress in 1910.

On May 12, 1909, Charles Sheldon married Louisa Gulliver, the daughter of a wealthy and socially prominent Manhattan lawyer. He was forty-one, she twelve years his junior. A big-city girl with a finishing-school education, Louisa was athletic and loved the out-of-doors. An accomplished horsewoman, she preferred riding to parties, and could drive a four-in-hand team with skill.

For their honeymoon, Charles Sheldon took his bride to, of all places, Admiralty Island off the coast of Alaska to observe the huge grizzlies that abounded there. They camped in a tent amid drenching downpours and opaque fogs, occasionally venturing forth when weather permitted. If privacy was what they wanted, they got plenty of it. Sheldon described one incident that took place on the island in his book *The Wilderness of the North Pacific Coast Islands*. The newlyweds had found a place where the salmon were running and hid among some alders in hopes that bears would come to the creek in search of fish. Here the couple sat, in drizzling rain, awaiting developments:

> We were seated about three feet apart, in front of a large
> spruce tree, with rifles across our knees, when Mrs. Sheldon,

turning her head to the left, discovered a large male bear standing motionless in the alders exactly *six feet* away, with ears cocked forward, intently watching her. . . . Her quick motion, as she turned to me, frightened it, and with a sudden jump backward it disappeared in the brush.

Although his bear watching might sound a little reckless, Sheldon by this time had had a great deal of experience with grizzlies under all kinds of conditions. Never had he been threatened by a bear. Even wounded bears and females with cubs always tried to flee. Sheldon was convinced that the great bears were extremely shy around humans and viewed reports of aggressive bears with suspicion. Convinced that most bear-attack stories were either exaggerations or reports of confused animals that ran toward humans by mistake, he had no fear of grizzlies.

The Sheldons made their home in New York and enjoyed the cultural amenities offered by the city. Charles loved music, and they often attended concerts and the opera, but they tended to avoid the social whirl to which they had entrée. Carolyn, their first child, was born in 1911; a son, William, in 1912; Louisa in 1913; and their last child, Eleanor, arrived in 1915. Despite having been a bachelor for so long, Sheldon found that married life agreed with him. He would continue to undertake collecting trips for the Biological Survey, but they would now be of shorter duration than his epic northern journeys.

Revolution had broken out in Mexico in November 1910, and the unrest soon spread to the state of Chihuahua. A New York newspaper contacted Sheldon to get his reaction. Sheldon responded that there had been flare-ups of this kind many times before, and that this one would probably subside as had previous disturbances. His friend Enrique Creel was governor of Chihuahua, and Sheldon thought that men of his caliber could well handle the situation. Sheldon was wrong, of course. Within a few months President Porfirio Díaz was forced to flee the country; Creel and Luis Terrazas soon followed suit. After spending a decade in the United States, both of them returned to Chihuahua in the early 1920s.

Up until the time of the revolution, the El Potosí mine had been paying its owners handsome profits, but now American investments in Mexico were in dire jeopardy. Sheldon eventually succeeded in selling his shares in the mine, but exactly when and how is unclear. According to Leonard Sanford, he held on to his shares "through thick and thin," and did not unload them until the early 1920s. Although many foreigners with Mexican holdings lost their investments, not all did. The policy of nationalizing large private and foreign-owned properties in Mexico was applied gradually. The Hearst family, for example, maintained ownership of the Babicora Ranch until 1953, when it was sold to the Mexican government and broken up into small peasant settlements called *ejidos*.

Early in 1915, Charles and Louisa Sheldon, accompanied by Edward Nelson, traveled to Chihuahua to visit old friends and, presumably, to check on the status of the El Potosí. The revolution was then going full blast, but the United States had maintained a position of neutrality during the conflict, and Americans could still visit Mexico in relative safety. This changed with Pancho Villa's raid on Columbus, New Mexico, in March 1916, and the subsequent punitive incursion into Mexico by the U.S. Army. Anti-American feelings were inflamed by the presence of foreign troops on Mexican soil, and Americans were there after wise to stay home. In February 1921, after most of the fighting was over, Sheldon traveled to Chihuahua alone. On this trip he took a horseback ride into the Sierra Madre, but he did no hunting or collecting. His main purpose appears to have been business, and it is likely that he divested himself of his mining shares at this time. He never returned to Chihuahua again.

Sheldon's first book, *The Wilderness of the Upper Yukon*, was published in 1911. Theodore Roosevelt, now a contributing editor for *The Outlook* magazine, reviewed the book in an editorial entitled "The American Hunter-Naturalist." He described Sheldon and his book:

Mr. Charles Sheldon is a . . . wilderness wanderer, who to the hardihood and prowess of the old-time hunter adds the capacity of a first-class field naturalist, and, also, what is just as important, the power of literary expression. Such a man can do for the lives of the wild creatures of the wooded and mountainous wilderness what John Muir has done for the physical features of the wilderness. . . . His experiences in Alaska, and indeed in the entire Northwest, are such as no other man has had; and no other writer on the subject has ever possessed both his power of observation and his power of recording vividly and accurately what he has seen. . . . In short, this volume is one of the rare volumes which should be in the library of every man who cares for stories of adventure.

The book was the last word on northern wild sheep for decades. In 1974, outdoor journalist and big-game hunter Jack O'Connor called it the "definitive book on the color variations and distribution among Stone and Dall sheep. It is uncannily accurate." Sheldon's *The Wilderness of the North Pacific Coast Islands* came out in 1912, and while well received, it did not have the lasting impact of the earlier book devoted primarily to mountain sheep. His most famous work, *The Wilderness of Denali*, which described his remarkable Alaskan adventures, was not published until after his death.

When the Boone and Crockett Club formed its permanent Game Preservation Committee in 1911, Grinnell was appointed chairman and Sheldon a member. Sheldon succeeded Grinnell as chairman the following year, and for many years he virtually worked full time on conservation causes. One of the first of these projects was a successful campaign to establish the National Elk Refuge at Jackson Hole, Wyoming. In 1913, Congress passed club-supported legislation bringing coherence and uniformity to waterfowl regulations by placing migratory birds under federal jurisdiction.

But the cause that Sheldon thought the most urgent was saving the pronghorn antelope from extinction. Before settlement, tens of millions of these fleet and graceful animals roamed the West's prairies and deserts. In 1908, Dr. T. S. Palmer of the Biological Survey calculated that only 20,000 pronghorn survived in the United States and Canada. And, not only had the pronghorn been extirpated from large areas of their former range, their numbers were still declining. Sheldon and the Boone and Crockett Club worked feverishly to get western states to protect the pronghorn. This effort came to fruition when Oregon closed the season on pronghorn antelope in 1913 – the animal was now totally protected from hunting north of Mexico.

In the meantime, the club had undertaken a program to restore pronghorn to some of their former range. In 1911 the club had funded the capture of a small number of antelope in Yellowstone National Park. Some of these animals were shipped to the National Bison Range in Montana, and the remainder were sent to the Wichita Mountain National Wildlife Preserve in Oklahoma. Sheldon and the Boone and Crockett Club urged Congress to create new refuges specifically for pronghorn, and offered to raise the money to fence and stock them. Sheldon wrote:

> After the bison, it [pronghorn], more than any other game, is associated with the romance and development of the early West. If heroic efforts are not made to save it, this generation will be responsible for the crime of its extermination. The Committee therefore has concentrated its efforts toward saving and increasing the antelope.

Under Sheldon's leadership, the Boone and Crockett Club financed other transplants. In 1914, thirteen pronghorn were purchased from Alberta and shipped to Wind Cave National Park in South Dakota. Additional animals were sent to the National Bison Range and other refuges. But all of the early reintroductions were failures. No one knew what conditions had to be met for transplanted antelope to prosper, and many mistakes were made. The numbers of animals trapped and transplanted were always too few, and once at their destination, the animals were restricted to small, fenced pastures where they were vulnerable to predators. Other transplant attempts using newly born fawns were also fraught with problems. The results had been very discouraging, and in 1921, Sheldon wrote Edward Nelson, "Personally, I believe that the antelope are doomed, yet every attempt should be made to save them."

Unknown to anyone, however, the pronghorn was on the verge of making a comeback. Under Edward Nelson's leadership, a census of all known pronghorn populations was conducted from 1922 to 1924. The Biological Survey reported that there were about 28,000 pronghorn in twelve states and two Canadian provinces. Another 2,000 to 2,500 antelope still resided in Mexico, and although the status of the animal remained critical, they had increased from the 1908 estimate. The trend was upward. Although the early transplants had not succeeded, the legal protection given the antelope had produced the desired effect. Today, approximately 1.3 million pronghorn roam the American West. That this animal did not go over the brink to extinction is due to the pioneering efforts of men like Charles Sheldon.

Growing family and conservation responsibilities meant a shrinking commitment to zoological collecting. Sheldon did not give up his work for the Biological Survey entirely, however. In 1912 and again in 1913 he hunted bighorn sheep in Arizona, and in 1915, 1916, and 1921 he expanded his inventory of mountain sheep to include Sonora, Mexico. It is the accounts of these expeditions, transcribed from his journals, that are presented in this volume. Although not as extensive as his northern ramblings, his desert hunts were no less daring and physically demanding. These southwestern journals, besides conveying all of the joys of discovering fascinating new landscapes, are the more powerful because they were written by an older Sheldon who was now a seasoned field naturalist.

In the spring of 1915, the U.S. government announced a plan to build a railroad connecting Fairbanks, Alaska, with Seward on the coast. Construction was to start immediately. Few Americans paid much attention to this distant project, but Sheldon reacted with alarm. The railroad would pass near the eastern edge of his proposed Denali National Park and bring hunters and prospectors into the area. Sheldon contacted every conservation leader and influential politician he knew, asking them to support his park plan. The response was now enthusiastic, as railroads were well known to be associated with vanishing wildlife. Sheldon went to Washington and found a strong ally in

Stephen Mather, the assistant secretary of the interior in charge of national parks. While in Washington, he contacted James Wickersham, Alaska's representative in Congress, and lobbied him on behalf of the park. Alaska's governor was also courted, and Sheldon found remarkably little opposition to his park proposal. It was difficult to argue that Mount McKinley was not worthy of national park status.

In 1916, Congress passed legislation creating the National Park Service, a professional bureau charged with managing the nation's park system. Its first chief was Sheldon's ally, Stephen Mather. In the fall of that year, Sheldon moved his family permanently to Washington so that he could maintain close contact with as many government officials as possible. His work was paying off. Congressman Wickersham introduced Sheldon's bill in the House, and Senator Kay Pittman of Nevada introduced a companion bill in the Senate. With the active support of the new and aggressive park service, legislation creating a 2,200-square-mile Mount McKinley National Park was passed on February 19, 1917. On February 26, Charles Sheldon personally took the bill to the White House, where President Woodrow Wilson signed it into law. After the signing, the president handed the pen to Sheldon.

Money to staff the new park was not immediately forthcoming, however. Funds were not appropriated to administer the park until 1921, when, at Sheldon's urging, Harry Karstens was hired as the park's first superintendent. He served in this capacity until 1928, when he resigned to return to private life. Karstens died in 1955.

Elated over the establishment of his national park and the wildlife protection it would afford, Sheldon was nonetheless unhappy with the park's name. He wrote:

> "*Denali*, The High One"; "*Sultana*, His Wife"; the former more sublime perhaps than any other mountain in the world. The Indians who have lived for countless generations in the presence of these colossal mountains have given them names that are both euphonious and appropriate. . . . Can it be denied that the names they gave to the most imposing features of

their country should be preserved? Can it be too late to make an exception to current geographic rules and restore these beautiful names – names so expressive of the mountains themselves, and so symbolic of the Indians who bestowed them?

The names of Mount McKinley and its slightly lower companion peak Mount Foraker have not been changed, but the name of the park was changed to Denali National Park in 1980. Not far from the site of Sheldon's winter cabin a plaque honors him as the park's founder, and next to it, a second commemorates Harry Karstens's tenure as superintendent. The park has been enlarged several times and now encompasses about 9,400 square miles.

When America declared war on Germany in April 1917, Theodore Roosevelt offered to raise a regiment of volunteers and lead them into battle. Sheldon told him that, should such a regiment be formed, he could be counted on to volunteer. Wisely, the secretary of war declined the old Rough Rider's offer. Roosevelt's sons, however, were soon at the front, and his youngest, Quentin, died in the war. Sheldon's Yukon hunting companion Frederick Selous, although in his mid-sixties, was also killed fighting the Germans and defending the Empire in East Africa. Sheldon, now nearly fifty and with five dependents, spent the war years as an unpaid volunteer in the Office of Naval Intelligence in Washington. On January 16, 1919, shortly after the armistice, Roosevelt unexpectedly died in his sleep. He was only sixty years old, and his sudden death was a great personal loss to Sheldon.

Sheldon's successful campaign for Mount McKinley National Park was followed by a painful episode that also involved Alaska. As America geared up for the Great War, there were enormous political pressures to relax recently imposed restrictions on the use of public lands and increase the production of natural resources to help the war effort. Proposals were made to increase grazing on the national forests, to open the national parks to livestock, to accelerate timber cutting, and to again allow game to be sold commercially. Some of these measures were approved, and conservationists saw their hard-earned gains vanishing in a wave of war hysteria. As an example, the new Alaska delegate to Congress, Charles Sulzer, introduced a bill drastically liberalizing Alaska's game code. The territory had been chafing under federal game laws passed in 1902 and 1908, and although generous by today's standards, these regulations were considered too strict by many Alaskans. Wartime conditions had caused the price of beef to rise steeply, and Alaskan officials were increasingly ignoring the illegal killing and selling of game meat. For all practical purposes, Alaska now had no game code, and Sulzer's legislation would only ratify the existing situation.

Edward Nelson, now chief of the Biological Survey, and Sheldon were brought in to discuss the Sulzer bill because of their experience in Alaska. The men met with Sulzer, expressed their concerns, and the bill was modified. Sheldon was especially worried about Alaska's grizzlies and mountain sheep, two species that everywhere melted away under heavy hunting. The compromise legislation would ease the restrictions on the hunting of moose and caribou, the principal species used for food, and maintain tighter controls on the taking of bears and sheep. Sulzer convinced Nelson and Sheldon that this compromise was the most conservative law that Alaskans would accept.

When animal protection advocate William T. Hornaday read Sulzer's compromise bill with its more liberal bag limits, he exploded in vitriolic fury. Moreover, he viciously attacked Nelson and Sheldon for going along with it, despite the fact that they had known each other for years and had worked together on several wildlife-related issues. Hornaday, director of the New York Zoological Park (Bronx Zoo), was a vociferous proponent of game protection and he was not about to hold his tongue. In 1912 a group of wealthy patrons that included Henry Ford and Andrew Carnegie endowed the Permanent Wildlife Protection Fund for the purpose of supporting Hornaday's conservation work. Hornaday was free to use the proceeds from the fund as he saw fit, and this independence seems to have made him a bit reckless.

Sheldon and Hornaday had been allies but not friends. The two men had totally different personalities. Sheldon was scholarly, reserved, and self-effacing, preferring to let others have the limelight. Hornaday, however, was bombastic and combative and was never happier than when engaged in a rough-and-tumble row. Nonetheless, once his mind was made up, Sheldon was just as tenacious and strong-willed as his feisty colleague.

Hornaday carried the day in the fight over the Sulzer bill and it was killed in Congress in 1918. The bill's defeat did not really trouble Sheldon—he had supported it reluctantly, trying to make the best of a bad situation. But Hornaday's personal attacks on Sheldon's character and motives resulted in bitter feelings that were never forgotten. Undaunted by this personal acrimony, Sheldon continued to quietly work for a better game code for his beloved Alaska. After consulting with regional experts, conservationists, and wildlife biologists, he patiently formulated a comprehensive new set of game regulations for the territory. This new game code, which was enacted by Congress in 1924 and took effect in 1925, was a model of progressive game legislation. Versions of it were adopted throughout the United States, and it served, without serious modification, to meet the needs of Alaska's wildlife through to statehood.

The Sheldon family had always summered at Woodstock, Vermont, not far from Rutland. But in 1919, Charles heard about a wilderness lodge operated by an American at Lake Kedgemakooge (Kejimkujik on some maps) in the interior of western Nova Scotia. He made a quick visit to inspect the place and liked what he saw. For the next several years the Sheldons spent their summers at Kedgemakooge. The main lodge was simple, but offered excellent meals. About two dozen widely spaced cabins were scattered around one end of the lake, one of the largest in Nova Scotia. Sheldon rented two of the rustic cabins, one for the children and one for the adults.

The country around Lake Kedgemakooge was pristine forest with numerous streams and smaller lakes—fabulous canoe country. Sheldon had two canoes custom-made to his specifications out of canvas and wood, and the family kept them in constant use. Beaver and moose were common. Caribou had been exterminated years earlier, but the introduced white-tailed deer

Charles Sheldon and his children at Lake Kedgemakooge, Nova Scotia, 1919. Left to right, Eleanor, Carolyn, William, and Louisa. Courtesy Eleanor Sheldon Lunde.

were becoming abundant. Every stream and pond was full of trout, and the fly fishing was superb.

While on a canoe trip several miles from the cabins, Charles Sheldon discovered a small lake of exquisite beauty. Unlike many of the small lakes on the island, which tend to be boggy and slightly discolored by peat, this one was spring fed and crystal clear. Sheldon named it Beaver Lake and each summer pitched two lean-to tents on the pond's shore. Using the skills he had learned as a youth, he built a large, elaborate stone fireplace in front of each tent. To protect the surrounding area from logging, he leased several hundred acres around the lake from the Nova Scotia government. The Sheldons thus spent much of each summer camped in their private wilderness away from the cabins. Today, the lands around Lake Kedgemakooge and Beaver Lake are a national park.

Years after their father's death, the Sheldon children wrote reminiscences about him, and they all focus on those idyllic summers in Nova Scotia. It makes one envious to read them. The days were filled with outdoor adventures, canoeing, fishing, swimming, their father always on hand to identify a bird or a track or a wildflower. William Sheldon recalled that his father had given him a .22 rifle, but had a strict ethic about shooting game – anything shot had to be put to use. Each squirrel, snowshoe hare, and woodchuck William bagged went into the stewpot, and their skins and skulls were prepared as specimens for study.

It is not surprising that all of Charles Sheldon's children developed a deep love for nature and the out-of-doors. Two of them became well-known naturalists. Carolyn became interested in small mammals and developed into an authority on jumping mice of the genus *Zapus*, publishing several papers on these little rodents. Later, William followed in his father's footsteps and when only eighteen collected sheep and other animals in western Canada. After graduating from Yale in 1933, he accompanied an expedition to China in search of the giant panda. William served with distinction during World War II and was awarded the Bronze Star for valor on five occasions. After the war he earned a Ph.D. in biology at Cornell University and headed the Cooperative Wildlife Research Unit at the University of Massachusetts until his retirement in 1972. He was the author of *The Book of the American Woodcock*, which was published in 1967. It is still the definitive work on this unusual game bird. Three of the children, Carolyn (1911–1973), William (1912–1987), and Louisa (1913–1973), suffered from a form of muscular dystrophy later in adult life. Only Eleanor (1915–) escaped the debilitating effects of this inherited ailment.

When in Washington, the Sheldons lived quietly during the Roaring Twenties. Charles continued to add to his impressive library, concentrating on works relating to hunting, exploration, and natural history. Over the years he had acquired many rare volumes from around the world. Theodore Roosevelt, a great lover of books, once remarked that Sheldon's collection was "the choicest sporting library in the country." His more than six thousand volumes were eventually acquired by Yale University, and in 1930, John C. Phillips compiled a 639-page catalogue of the Sheldon library for the Boone and Crockett Club.

The Sheldon home was always open to roving naturalists and explorers. Edward Nelson, a bachelor, spent a lot of time there, and other visitors included the pioneer aviator Richard Byrd and Norwegian explorer Roald Amundsen. Sheldon's own explorations ceased after his 1921–1922 journey to Seriland. This grueling trip had taken its toll on his stamina, and he knew it was time to give up such strenuous work.

In 1926 a flap erupted involving Amundsen that had just about everyone in America taking sides. The famous leader of the first expedition to reach the South Pole was in the United States to address a meeting of the National Geographic Society. His appearance carried with it a large honorarium of several thousand dollars. A few days before he was to address the society, Amundsen visited his old friend Frederick Cook, who had accompanied him on one of his early expeditions. Cook had fallen on hard times—he was serving a sentence for securities fraud in the federal penitentiary at Fort Leavenworth, Kansas. After meeting with Cook, Amundsen was interviewed by the press, and his remarks were reported in such a way as to imply that he sided with Cook in his old dispute with Peary as to who was the first to reach the North Pole. Robert Peary had become an American hero of immense stature, had been made an admiral, and since his death in 1920 had almost been canonized as a saint.

The instant that Amundsen's comments appeared in the newspapers, the society canceled his address. Amundsen protested that he had been misquoted, but to no avail. He was hurt and embarrassed by the cancellation, and, moreover, he needed the money. Sheldon discussed the matter with Amundsen and concluded that his friend had been ill treated. Sheldon wrote several letters to Dr. Gilbert Grosvenor, president of the National Geographic Society, on Amundsen's behalf, but the organization was adamant. Sheldon then resigned from the society.

From 1924 to 1929, the National Conference on Outdoor Recreation met in Washington for several days each spring. The purpose of the conference was to formulate an outdoor recreation policy for the U.S. government. All forms of recreation were to be studied and discussed, from bear hunting to golf. Delegates included leaders from all facets of the American establishment—politicians, heads of government bureaus, business leaders, conservationists, academics, and union officials. The conference had been conceived and organized by Charles Sheldon. He sold his concept to his friend Theodore Roosevelt, Jr., assistant secretary of the navy, and he in turn promoted the idea in the Coolidge administration. Roosevelt chaired the initial conference, and Sheldon served on the executive committee and chaired several special committees formulating national wildlife policy.

National conferences of this kind are noted for accomplishing little of lasting importance, and in terms of immediate results, this one was perhaps not much different. But some of the committee resolutions, quite revolutionary at the time, were eventually adopted as government policy. The conference, for example, endorsed Aldo Leopold's idea for preserving portions of the national forests as wilderness. It also called for the establishment of a nationwide system of waterfowl refuges and public shooting areas. But the most important result of the conference was more subtle. Before the conference convened, outdoor recreation had been generally viewed as good, healthy exercise, but of no real national significance. After the conference filed its final reports, outdoor recreation was regarded by most Americans as an important, indeed essential, aspect of their culture.

Charles Sheldon died of a sudden heart attack at the family's cabin in Nova Scotia on September 21, 1928. He would have been sixty-one in less than a month. The funeral and burial were at Rutland, Vermont.

The next year, the Boone and Crockett Club, in cooperation with the National Audubon Society, raised $20,000 to buy 4,000 acres of private land in northwestern Nevada as the nucleus for a pronghorn sanctuary. It was decided that the refuge would be named for Charles Sheldon in recognition of his pioneering work on behalf of this animal. In 1931 the land purchased by the conservation organizations was turned over to the federal government, and together with 30,000 acres of adjacent public land, was designated by President Herbert Hoover as the Charles Sheldon National Antelope Refuge. In 1936, President Franklin Roosevelt, by executive order, enlarged the refuge to its present size of 575,000 acres.

Charles Sheldon about 1925. #75–42–2, William Sheldon Collection, Alaska and Polar Regions Department, University of Alaska, Fairbanks.

In the assessment of Charles Sheldon's many contributions to our nation's well-being, Denali National Park looms large as a lasting accomplishment. The hundreds of biological specimens he collected remain in the National Museum at the Smithsonian, continuously available to refine our understanding of North America's wildlife. His books have been read for decades. But his greatest contribution is less tangible. Parks and refuges have value only if future generations cherish and preserve them. Charles Sheldon did much to foster a conservation ethic in the hearts and minds of Americans. That is the most important legacy of his life and work.

CHARLES SHELDON'S QUEST FOR DESERT BIGHORN SHEEP
AND ADVENTURES WITH THE HAVASUPAI AND
SERI INDIANS

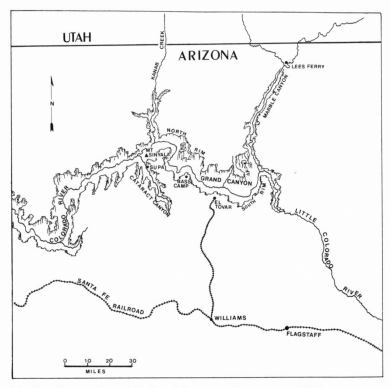

UTAH

ARIZONA

LEES FERRY

KANAB CREEK

MARBLE CANYON

NORTH RIM

MT SINYALA

SUPAI

BASS CAMP

GRAND CANYON

EL TOVAR

SOUTH RIM

CATARACT CANYON

COLORADO RIVER

LITTLE COLORADO RIVER

SANTA FE RAILROAD

WILLIAMS

FLAGSTAFF

N

0   10   20   30
MILES

Northern Arizona showing the Grand Canyon and environs ca. 1912.

1

HUNTING SHEEP WITH HAVASUPAIS IN THE GRAND CANYON, 1912

After surveying and collecting mountain sheep in the Canadian Yukon and Alaska (1904–1908), Charles Sheldon focused his attention on the sheep of Arizona and Sonora, Mexico. From 1912 to 1922 he mounted five expeditions to this region for the purpose of obtaining specimens of desert bighorn.

Sheldon's first collecting trip to the Southwest was a special one. Accompanied by his friend and mentor Edward W. Nelson of the U. S. Bureau of Biological Survey, he traveled by rail to the South Rim of the Grand Canyon in the fall of 1912. The two men were interested in obtaining a series of sheep specimens from the canyon, both rams and ewes, to determine if the Colorado River was a barrier separating two distinct forms of bighorn. Although this was Sheldon's first trip to Arizona, Nelson was no newcomer to either the state or the canyon. He had lived on a cattle ranch near Springerville in the 1880s and had collected birds on the North Rim of the Grand Canyon in 1909.

The naturalists were met at El Tovar, the elegant lodge built by the Santa Fe Railroad Company in 1905, by William Bass and his daughter, Edith. Bass operated a much more modest camp for tourists on the South Rim a few miles west of El Tovar. The Basses guided Sheldon and Nelson down into the Grand Canyon by way of a side drainage called Cataract Canyon to Supai, the remote village of the Havasupai Indians. William and Edith Bass then returned to Bass Camp, leaving Sheldon and Nelson in the care of the Havasupais. Sheldon made arrangements with two Indian men to go with him deeper into the Grand Canyon in search of sheep, and Nelson, an older man, remained near Supai to collect birds and care for any specimens that might be procured.

In 1893, President Benjamin Harrison, by executive order, withdrew much of the Grand Canyon from the public domain and incorporated it into the federal forest reserve system. In 1906, President Theodore Roosevelt signed a bill making the canyon a game preserve. Two years later he issued a proclamation declaring the canyon to be a national monument. In 1919 Congress passed legislation creating Grand Canyon National Park.

Based on the animals collected by Sheldon and others, taxonomists now consider bighorn sheep on both sides of the Colorado River as belonging to a single subspecies. This is not surprising, as ewes and young rams are good swimmers and have been known to cross the Colorado River during times of low water. Mature rams are less able to cross the river, because their heavy horns make it difficult to keep their heads above water.

Nov. 16, 1912. We started from El Tovar at 11 a.m. and drove for 5 hours across the piñon belt to Bass Camp. Bass' daughter, 16 years old, rode, leading a saddle horse. We met a few Supai [Havasupai] Indians—some of the squaws were hunting piñon nuts. I saw pack rat sign, here and there a few gopher diggings, Woodhouse's jays [scrub jays], Rocky Mountain jays [Clark's nutcrackers], and a few flocks of piñon jays, also a red-tailed hawk, a few snowbirds [juncos], and flickers. The road was fairly good, and the last 5 miles was near and in places along the rim of the canyon. Bass Camp is a comfortable small house. There are several trails along the rim of the canyon here. Deer are very scarce near the canyon, and antelope are rarely seen. On the whole, animal life is scarce, except for *peromyscus* mice. Weather clear, some wind, chilly.

Nov. 17. All the morning was lost by Bass looking for horses. He came back and sent his daughter out, who returned at 12:30 not having found them. I looked the canyon over for sheep, but saw none. Taking the shotgun, I killed two titmice. I saw chickadees, also a white-belted [white-breasted] nuthatch.

We started and drove for 3½ hours across the same piñon country, finding and picking up a horse on the way. Bass' daughter came along. We descended a canyon for two or three miles and came to a government stable, which Bass broke into. We met Young (a teacher) and Frick, government health inspector of Indians. As we came into the canyon, old huts and camps of Indians appeared. I saw ravens, flickers, and snowbirds. Jays are common on the opposite side of this canyon, but not on this side. I saw the fresh tracks of blacktail deer at

A Havasupai dwelling. E. W. Nelson.

this end of the trail. We sleep tonight on the side of a hill in an old Indian camp. It is good to again see the brilliant night sky.

Nov. 18. We left after nine, Nelson and I taking the lead. Bass' daughter, Edith, came along leading a burro and a packhorse. At first we went down a very steep zigzag trail, and then down through a side canyon for two hours, then down Cataract Canyon. At a mile above Supai, a river [Havasu Creek] suddenly bursts from underground and flows in good volume downward, all the way between perpendicular cliffs several hundred feet high, turreted and castellated, all of sandstone. It was a wonderful 4-hour ride to Supai Village. I saw snowbirds all the way down, bushtits, Woodhouse's jay, rock and canyon wrens, also one *Citellus* [ground squirrel].

Bass and daughter left in the p.m. I arranged to have Jasper (a man of 26, son of the chief and probably future chief) come with me, also a lovable old Indian, Sinyala, an old hunter. More about Supai Village later. Weather warmer.

Sinyala (leading) and Jasper, with Mount Sinyala, a noted landmark in the Havasupai country, in the background. Charles Sheldon.

Nov. 19. Jasper had his horse packed at 9:45 a.m. and we started, taking bread, tea, sugar, rice, bacon, and flour. Sinyala met us with his horse and rifle and dog. I made him send the dog back and take back his rifle. We started immediately up the sandstone wall, the trail winding along the wall, rising higher and higher to the head of a canyon that joins Cataract Canyon at Supai. The trail was very rough and rocky and in places very dangerous. We reached the head of the canyon in two hours. Near the top I saw an old sheep track. Sinyala rode after reaching the top. Then we swung around just below the talus of the main rim, crossing numerous canyons at their heads for two more hours, then lunched. Then we continued the same way for two hours more, three or four miles around into the Grand Canyon, and camped southeast of a big lone mountain.

At noon, Jasper jumped on his horse behind the 125-lb. pack and continued all the rest of the day on the small unshod animal, which had been badly gashed by a wire fence. I saw bluebirds and rock and canyon wrens. Several Indian horses run about near the talus slopes. My feet got very sore in shoes, so later I put on moccasins, which were a relief. I find I still love to tramp. Sinyala's dog finally took the trail and caught us.

Tonight I am sitting between these two Indians, writing by firelight under a clear sky, the wonderful cliffs of the rim almost surrounding me, the big lone mountain in the distance, beyond which is the Grand Canyon. More about the country when I know it better. Very windy in the p.m. I am thinking of the loved ones at home.

Nov. 20. It began to rain early this a.m., and we moved camp 1/4 mile to a cave. After eating, both Indians wanted to go hunting with me, but I said I would rather go alone. But Sinyala mounted his horse and started with me. We tramped for two hours down toward the Colorado River to where he said the sheep are found. I saw an old coyote track, rarely a gopher digging, and canyon and rock wrens.

I found that there is a basin below cliffs near the river, and but one place to descend with a rope. Then, after covering this basin of half a mile, you are shut off from going farther down by more high cliffs. We went over at the risk of life. I saw but one old sheep track. It seems that this is the only spot the Indians hunt, and when a sheep is seen they sometimes get it. I saw several well-worn trails below, close to the river. Sheep undoubtedly live along the river, easily going down in numerous places to drink. It is a vast territory for them, and the canyons below are a wonderful sight. I saw no sheep, not a sign on the rim of these cliffs, and there is but one place to get them. Sinyala got tired after lunch and rode back. I followed the cliff rim all the p.m., but saw nothing but trails low down.

Tonight the wind is howling and blowing the sand in clouds over us. We have no frying pan or plates, and I am living like an Indian. The Indians call this lone mountain "Week-eel-eela," which they say means "stick sitting up," a general term for butte [later officially named Mount Sinyala by the U.S. Geographic Board at Sheldon's suggestion]. The chances for sheep look slim unless I can find a territory to hunt. Weather perfect.

Bighorn habitat in the inner gorge of the Grand Canyon. Charles Sheldon.

Nov. 21. We packed early and went easterly for an hour and a half to a spring where two canyons head. Sinyala went down the rim of the canyon with Jasper, and I waited until he came back. Jasper signaled us to approach and we went down toward him. We descended a very steep, dangerous, rocky, cliffy canyon, and when near the bottom, fresh ewe tracks were abundant. At once I made Sinyala sit down, and went forward. Soon I saw a ewe (small) 200 yards up on the slope, and with sight up I killed her with the second shot. Then going forward again, keeping low in the bottom, I saw two ewes coming toward me. I kept low until they appeared, 75 yards away, running. A shot killed one and a second shot hit the other which staggered on until I fired again and killed her. Then I saw another, 300 yards up, under the cliffs of the rim. Putting up the sight, the first two shots went under her as she moved about in confusion. Then holding a coarse sight as she stood on a rock, I killed her.

I beckoned to Sinyala and went forward, and around a corner saw two large rams high up under a cliff, in a good place to stalk. I started and was nearly in shot [within range] when I saw

Sinyala holding Charles Sheldon's rifle. Charles Sheldon.

both run and heard the dog, Tip, barking. They ran toward the
deep canyon, the second this side of the bottom, and went over.
Before I could get there the larger one ran out. I hurried forward

and saw a large ram 25 feet below, standing on a foot-wide projection with 2,000 feet of precipice directly below. He was cornered. I pulled out the Kodak and started toward him, but he turned and ran. I waited until he got back from the brink and fired and hit his hindquarter. He fell and rose, and I killed him. I saw another ewe and then two more, very near—100 yards—but did not shoot.

We finally had a large ram! After photographing and measuring, we skinned him. It was moonlight (nearly full) when we finished. Both Indians were loaded with meat and we started climbing down to the ewes below. I measured them and took out their entrails. Then the dangerous walk of two miles up the canyon. The full moon was all that made it possible. I looked back soon after starting—the moon was to my right, its light bathing the canyon walls. Beyond, the rim was struck by the last rays of the setting sun. Very beautiful.

At nine we reached the top, then food and tea. The big ram's ears are completely rotten on the inside from ticks. The bottom of the canyon we went down is 2,000 feet below. Then a box canyon with perpendicular walls 1,500 or 2,000 feet high leads to the Colorado. The Indians call the Colorado "Hak-a-tay-a." Too tired to write more tonight. The success of today has been wonderful. Weather perfect.

Nov. 22. I was warm, too warm, under the robe last night. Early we all went down the canyon to prepare the sheep. I found ticks in the ears of all, but more in the big ram's. I left the Indians to take the skins off the ewes, and went on to try to find other big rams.

I walked along the cliffs clear to the Colorado River, and down it 2 miles. I saw 3 big rams on the opposite side and a ram 75 yards away on the far bank, but would not shoot. I saw three ewes and 5-year-old and 3-year-old rams on my side, and stalked within shot, but could not find big rams. Sheep tracks are all over, but no well-defined trails except one, and that high. I saw faint trails on both terraces below along the river.

Canyon and rock wrens were seen, and a bird, small as a phoebe, sitting on the top of an agave stalk—blackish head above, blacker back, primaries, wing coverts, and tail, white throat and grayish breast and belly—some kind of a flycatcher [a black phoebe]. Yellow is the most common flower color. Bisnaga [barrel cactus] is prominent everywhere, also prickly pear. *Echinocactus* is less conspicuous. Agave or mescal is everywhere.

Besides the magnificent views of perpendicularly walled canyons and cliffs, I was most impressed with the profound silence—not a breath of wind today, not a sound, not a rustle of grass or weeds, not an insect murmur, not a falling rock. Silence absolute. Only my lifelong habit of hearing insects kept the sound in my imagination.

I came up the canyon by moonlight—full moon—wonderfully beautiful. The Indians had all the skins and most of the meat here. These terraces rise from the cliff rims, with a grass-grown talus slope above each. I am on the third terrace, where the sheep mostly feed, that is when not in the bottom of the canyon. Pack rat houses are common, gopher diggings scarce. Weather perfect.

Nov. 23. For three days there has not been a breath of wind, not a cloud. The sun at midday is fairly hot, but it is always cool when one is in the shadow. Soon after daylight I tied up the skins and sent Jasper to Supai with them so that Nelson can look after them. I started down the canyon directly west of camp, seeing a fox track in the bottom. There is a fine spring at the bottom, and I visited two old Indian camps. A few old sheep tracks were noticed as I was on my way to the Colorado River. I went down the west side of the canyon and down the river four miles—very rough walking. I saw a five-year-old ram with a three-year-old, also three ewes. All could have been easily stalked. I saw three ewes across the river and again four ewes.

I had gone too far and, returning, darkness was about to catch me. In going down a canyon, I had to creep along cliffs on the east side where the moonlight does not reach. I started back down the east side of this canyon and reached the Colorado and went a mile north. There were plenty of sheep tracks. The moon rose and was full. I tramped along the brink of a canyon, enjoying the wonderful effect of the moon lighting up the walls of the canyon and, here and there, making the water shine in the depths below. I had to tramp up to the heads of canyons, on, on, some of the slopes full of boulders and broken rock. The slope of the canyon was very steep and I had to use the greatest caution. Again, not a breath of wind. The roar of the river below and the moonlit crests of the rim made it a strange, unique experience.

At 12 midnight I reached the foot of the east canyon, and being very tired made tea. Then, with moccasins full of holes, tramped up, reaching camp at 2 a.m. I noticed fox tracks in one place today, a big ram I did not see. I went directly to sleep without eating. Most of the sheep are along the Colorado River and the slopes of the big tributaries. Perfect weather.

Nov. 24. Early I took Sinyala to show me the country up the east canyon. It is interesting to go with him—he knows every foot of the country. He showed me blinds near the rim where "a long time ago Indians used to lie and shoot sheep as they passed from the head of one canyon to that of another." We followed the rim and finally I located 3 ewes and watched them. Eventually one acted the "sentinel," in spite of not having done so for an hour and a half. The sheep here act exactly like all the northern sheep I have ever seen—very watchful and alert. I saw tracks, one track near the rim and another crossing the flat a mile from the rim, between canyons. Sheep (at least a few) probably go up to the rim when the snow melts to get green food which may not grow down in the canyon until later. I have only seen two lambs. There are no enemies of sheep here, except golden eagles. The bobcat is so scarce as to be negligible. Perhaps the eagles keep the sheep numbers down. The sheep do not gather in large bands, but they are all along the whole canyon. In this canyon, at least, the mountain sheep will live long after wapiti and other animals become extinct [the range occupied by elk in North America had shrunk drastically by 1912 and the outlook was bleak].

My short hunt is over. With more time I could get other large rams. It is a very dangerous country to hunt.

Nov. 25. We packed and came without incident to the village. I rode a good part of the way, walking only around the canyon heads.

Nov. 26. Nelson and I and two Indians rode, with packhorses carrying our trophies, to the head of Cataract Canyon, where we passed the night, the Indian agent having accompanied us.

Nov. 27. The next a.m. we drove to El Tovar, and the same night I took the train directly to New York.

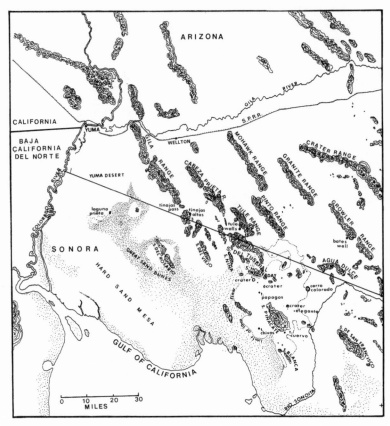

The desert sheep country of southwest Arizona and northwest Sonora. Adapted from Lumholtz, 1912.

2

ON THE ARIZONA-SONORA BORDER, 1913

In November 1913, Charles Sheldon set out to hunt mountain sheep in the Tinajas Altas and Tule mountains along the boundary between southwestern Arizona and northwestern Sonora, Mexico. Mountain sheep had been completely protected by law in Arizona Territory since 1893, but the new state game code now provided for the taking of sheep for scientific purposes. Mountain sheep were not then protected in Mexico.

On his arrival by train at Wellton, Arizona, Sheldon was met by Edward A. Goldman, Win Proebstel, and Murray Chappel. Goldman, a protégé of Edward Nelson with twenty years of experience collecting for the U.S. Biological Survey in Mexico and Central America, was interested in obtaining a series of mammals from this especially arid portion of the Sonoran Desert. Proebstel and Chappel were local residents whom Sheldon had engaged to provide transportation and assist around camp. Proebstel, who had a mining claim in the Copper Mountains south of Wellton, had previously guided Kermit Roosevelt on a sheep hunt in the Mexican portion of the Tinajas Altas Mountains in August 1911. However, once in the sheep country Sheldon planned to hunt alone, as was his preference and custom.

Complicating the expedition was the Mexican Revolution, which had broken out in 1910 and was to continue with varying degrees of intensity for more than a decade. Fortunately, Pancho Villa's raid on Columbus, New Mexico, was still in the future, and relations between the two countries were as yet generally amiable. Both insurrectos and government forces often crossed the border to seek refuge in the United States when pressed too hard by the opposite side. Even though Sheldon and Goldman spoke fluent Spanish, the little party was taking some risk by crossing into Mexico. Certainly, the outcome of being in possession of a "visa" from the wrong side could be unpleasant. Hence, Sheldon's ability to converse with any Mexicans they might meet was a decided advantage.

Looking east from above the Tinajas Altas. Peter L. Kresan.

The hub of the collecting trip was the Tinajas Altas or "high tanks," a series of deep plunge pools or potholes worn in solid rock in a steep canyon. The tanks are replenished by runoff after infrequent rains. They are in the southern end of the Tinajas Altas Mountains, a range that extends southeast from the Gila Mountains to the Mexican border (Sheldon refers to the entire group as the Gila Mountains). Located about three miles north of the border, these tinajas (literally "large jars") were an important water source for

Teddybear chollas in the Tinajas Altas Mountains. E. A. Goldman.

Mexicans traveling between Sonora and Baja California. The aridity and difficulty of this trail led to it being called Camino del Diablo (Devil's Road).

Several notable explorers preceded Charles Sheldon and his party at the Tinajas Altas. Probably the first non-Indian to visit them was the Jesuit missionary Eusebio Kino, who is thought to have watered his horses there on his way to the Gila River in 1699. Dr. Edgar Mearns, a physician and naturalist attached to the International Boundary Commission, which was engaged in resurveying the U.S.-Mexico boundary, camped at Tinajas Altas in February 1894. He hunted sheep in the nearby mountains and bagged a young female for a specimen. Sheldon mentions encountering boundary monuments placed during this survey, which was completed in 1896. The ethnologist W. J. McGee visited the Tinajas Altas in 1900, and spent the summer of 1905 camped near the tanks hoping to regain his health. During his latter stay, McGee made numerous weather observations and killed two bighorn sheep for food (there are no deer in the Tinajas Altas Mountains). Although only two of the tanks still held water at the end of McGee's stay, no one has ever reported the tanks to be entirely dry.

A yuccalike Bigelow nolina. E. A. Goldman.

This trip was Sheldon's introduction to the Sonoran Desert. He remarks about the dryness of the land, and this was not merely an Easterner's reaction to what is always an arid region. The year of Sheldon's visit saw only 1.04 inches of rain falling at Yuma, the nearest weather station. The average annual rainfall at Yuma is 3.4 inches.

The names, both common and scientific, of some of the plants mentioned by Sheldon have changed over the years. He uses the old spelling "sahuaro" for the saguaro cactus, and often refers to the plant as simply "giant cactus";

Sonoran Desert vegetation along a wash near Copper Mountain. E. A. Goldman.

Tinajas Altas Mountains seven miles north of the tanks. The small cactus in the foreground is a teddybear cholla. E. A. Goldman.

Grave of a traveler. Tinajas Altas gorge in the background. E. A. Goldman.

barrel cacti are called by their Mexican name, "bisnaga." The cactus that
"grabs" his attention the most is the teddybear cholla, known as Bigelow
cholla in Sheldon's day. This plant has spines so dense that it has a mislead-
ingly soft, furry appearance, hence its modern name. In reality, the spines are
incredibly sharp and possessed of tiny barbs that make their removal from
one's flesh a difficult and painful procedure. The stems or joints also come
loose from the plant with incredible ease and cling to any man or beast that
comes into contact with them.

The plant that Sheldon calls a yucca is the Bigelow nolina, a stem suc-
culent like the yucca, but actually a species of beargrass. In general appearance this nolina closely resembles the common soaptree yucca so widely dis-
tributed throughout the Southwest. Both the Bigelow nolina and Bigelow
cholla were named for John Bigelow, a botanist who collected plants in Arizona in 1853 as a member of the Whipple railroad survey.

Brittlebush (Encelia farinosa) is mentioned often by Sheldon, but he
usually refers to it as simply Encelia. When in bloom, this low, rounded
shrub is one of the most attractive plants in the Sonoran Desert. Its bright
yellow flowers and silvery gray leaves brighten the landscape, especially in
spring. The Mexicans gave the plant the name incienso (incense) because of
the aromatic properties of its sap when burned. The plant's flower stalks are
also an important food for desert bighorn sheep.

The common name for the plant that Sheldon calls Elaphrium is elephant tree. It is a thornless, shrubby, tropical tree with aromatic leaves. The
name is derived from the thickened, gnarled trunks, which, with a little
imagination, resemble an elephant's trunk. This resemblance is more apparent in Mexican species than in the small specimens that occur in Arizona's
Sonoran Desert.

Two other small Sonoran Desert trees attracted Sheldon's attention: the
paloverde and the desert ironwood. The name of the former means "green
stick" in Spanish and refers to the tree's evergreen trunk and branches. Two
species of paloverde inhabit the Tinajas Altas region, the foothill paloverde
and blue paloverde; both are legumes with yellow flowers. The ironwood, as
its name implies, has dense, hard wood that makes the best of campfires.

Other plants in southwestern Arizona and northwestern Mexico were
familiar to Sheldon from his years in Chihuahua. Creosote bush, which he
often calls "greasewood," grows in various forms throughout the Chihuahuan,
Sonoran, and Mohave deserts. It is a thinly stemmed shrub with small, res-
inous, olive green leaves that produce a distinctive pungent odor after a rain.
The spiny, wandlike stems of the ocotillo would also have been familiar to
Sheldon, as would the mesquite tree, closely related varieties of both plants
being found in the Chihuahuan Desert.

Nov. 19, 1913. Rainy. I reached Wellton at 1 a.m., having
spent most of the day in Phoenix. E. A. Goldman met me at the
station and we slept in the house of the postmaster, Bob Gale.
Up early, we breakfasted with his family, then dressed in hunt-

Murray Chappel waters a horse at the lower pool at Tinajas Altas. E. A. Goldman.

ing clothes and packed my outfit. At 10:30 Win Proebstel and Murray Chappel (cook) appeared with a cart drawn by two horses, and two extra saddle horses. My outfit was loaded and we started at 1 p.m. in the rain, which continued until we camped.

We traveled for about five hours to Proebstel's camp at a claim in the Copper Mountains. I rode horseback the last half of the way, got soaked in the rain and was very cold. The whole Gila range rose in the west. The desert was not rich in vegetation, except along the washes—a little mesquite, plenty of ironwood, some palo verdes and *Atriplex* [saltbush], scattered sahuaros, now and then a bisnaga, also small chollas, brittle bush (*Encelia*), and other unusual plants. Near the mountains the vegetation was more dense and the sahuaros larger, so that the desert was more picturesque. At camp we made a large fire and the sky later cleared. The only birds seen were a phainopepla and sage sparrows. Distance traveled, 18 miles.

Nov. 20. We started about 10:30, having been delayed by the wagon breaking down, which we repaired with wire. I rode. We crossed the plains to the base of the Gila range, and then followed some wagon tracks south toward the Tinajas Altas. Phainopeplas were common and I saw a few sage sparrows and, nearing the tanks, a raven and a jack rabbit. I caught a baby horned toad.

Just as we were arriving at the tanks, we saw fresh tracks of men and horses, then smoke and some men who suddenly disappeared. We knew they were Mexicans and at once stopped and unhitched, not caring to bring the wagon nearer the tanks. I took two canteens and went over into the pocket and saw about 12 men, fully armed, sitting about a fire, making flour tortillas. Then, up against the side of the mountain, I saw seventeen or eighteen men and the same number of horses. I stepped up and greeted them, and an educated fellow came over from the upper crowd and asked who I was, etc. At once I explained in Spanish our object, knowing they were all revolutionists camping near the water. He seemed relieved and told me he wished to bring me up to the chief. This man was the secretary and his name was Francisco Mendoza.

I walked with him up to the commander, whose name was Gallego. He had no uniform but was a thick-set man of force and brains. I found that he and several of them spoke good English. I tried to talk with sympathy and tact, told them to go ahead as far as we were concerned, and asked about the revolution, etc. Soon I got into an interesting conversation and felt that I had won their good will. Mendoza wrote a letter permitting me to go over the border when I told them I wanted to, and Gallego signed it. He then sent a man up to the tanks who filled the canteens for me, and I came back to our wagon, picking up a nice bleached four- or five-year-old ram's head on the way.

After eating, I went back with Win, who brought the horses for water. I gave Gallego a 5-gallon water bag. Then I remained and had a most interesting conversation about the revolution. They are retreating from, but not running away from, a fight near Calexico. They are also bringing a load of ammunition which is hidden with eight or ten mules. It will be brought in later. They could not stay here, and left to get feed for their horses, six miles away. It was a highly picturesque crowd, all armed with Winchesters (I saw two or three Krags), with belts of cartridges around their waists and over their shoulders (all soft-nosed bullets). Some of the horses were good ones, some with terrible backs, and some nearly exhausted. I noticed a pair of field glasses in a saddlebag. They had a blanket apiece, several smooth boards for making tortillas, which seemed to be their exclusive food, with coffee. Some were middle class and able, and some sad-looking peons. All had canteens. When they rode off, about ten walked. They told me they had lost horses from lack of water, etc. They will go on to Tule Tanks and then to where they can get cattle. They told me that they could not trust a regular soldier and had all agreed that they must fight it out by themselves. When they conquered, they would disband the army and remake an army of the revolutionists. They told me of the many cruelties of the Federals, how they had cut out the testicles of one man, and how this treatment was the cause of the fighting.

Nov. 21. Overcast, calm, and warm. I started at daylight, went down half a mile and up a canyon. I saw old sheep dung and was surprised to see that the rams' dung pellets were so long. I tramped up the canyon and watched both sides until noon but saw nothing, nor any new sign—plenty of old. Then I took tea. I saw plenty of rock wrens, a few canyon wrens, phainopeplas, a flycatcher, and other birds not recognized.

Then I climbed the mountain and descended the other side, very steep and dangerous. Old sheep sign was everywhere. I then walked up canyons, and in one saw a three-year-old ewe but did not shoot her. She appeared as dark as a Stone sheep. Darkness overtook me and I tramped along the range until I felt horse tracks with my feet—I started up a canyon where they led. I tramped for three hours up a wash and through the range and finally reached camp after a hard day, my feet and legs full of cactus. More about sheep later, but it is glorious to be again in the mountains with all the beauty of the landscape and fascination of the crags. I saw great quantities of dung that Proebstel

Indian mortars near Tinajas Altas. E. A. Goldman.

says is that of the Gila monster [probably chuckwalla droppings].

Nov. 22. Overcast and windy. I left early, after examining a coyote which Goldman caught in a trap near the tanks. Last night a Mexican camped near the tanks and left early in the a.m. before we were up—another revolutionist. I went down the range, up the canyons, climbed the mountains and ridges, followed sheep trails, and continued clear around and lunched at Surveyor Tank. I then circled around in Mexico to almost the point I reached yesterday.

I did not see a sheep all day. There are plenty of old tracks and plenty of old sheep dung along the base of the mountains, sometimes a hundred yards out on the desert. There is no grass on the mountains and only a few magueys [agaves] high up and a species of yucca. Just before dark, Win came with an extra saddle horse, met me at Surveyor Tank, and we rode back in the dark.

Murray Chappel fills a water bag at Raven Tank. E. A. Goldman.

Nov. 23. Clear, windy. I went up a canyon north of camp, climbed all the side canyons and finally the crest of the mountain. Then I lunched, enjoying the vistas both east and west. Then I descended the west side of the range, hunted various canyons, and took the Yuma road and reached camp at dark. After we were lying down, a Mexican rode by to the tanks, and later another one—revolutionists, though these denied it. Not a sheep seen all day.

Nov. 24. Perfect, clear day. We decided to move camp eight miles north to Raven Tank. I started ahead on a horse, reached a canyon, tied the horse and went up, carefully hunting the side canyons. I lunched, then climbed the crest and accepted the danger of climbing along it. It is peaked and jagged, the slopes very steep, and some of the rock loose. Finally I sat down. A raven flew over my head and squawked. Then I heard a rock fall. I saw an average-sized ram 150 yards below, looking up at me. The sun was in my face and so shone on my rifle barrel that the sight was blurred. My shot missed. The ram rushed out of sight down the canyon, and came running up the slope on the other side. I turned up the sight and fired eight more times but did not touch him. I found that I had accidentally put up my sight to 500 yards, thus my bad luck.

I followed the ram but found no blood sign. Then I climbed up and down and finally came to camp by following the horse tracks, as Win had come and gotten my horse. This camp is in a wash in a beautiful place. Win goes to Wellton tomorrow to get more horse food. I saw a jack rabbit yesterday.

Nov. 25. Perfect day, clear and calm. I started early toward the south, soon turned up a canyon and started to climb to the head. I see sheep beds on most of the saddles of the main ridges and spurs. I even find ewe beds on the side slopes, well hidden in brush, and great numbers of beds in caves. Lizards, little ones, are common. Chuck-a-walla dung is everywhere in the rocks, high and low.

The climb was very difficult and when I reached the top it seemed impossible to get down. But I slung my rifle on my back and attempted it. It was more dangerous than I should try and several times I was in a tight place, but finally I accomplished it. Then I hunted up a canyon and made another climb to a high peak, another difficult one, and then worked my way along the jagged crest, delighting in the scenery—the rough crestlines, the broken canyons and precipitous mountains, the vast deserts stretching away with mountain ranges rising out of them. I then made tea. Then another dangerous descent, and up a canyon, again ascending to the main crest. Then down the other side,

Rugged bighorn sheep habitat in the Tinajas Altas Mountains. Charles Sheldon.

hunting a canyon, again returning over the top and hunting down a canyon, returning to camp after dark.

Plenty of sheep sign, but not a sheep have I seen all day. Goldman was on the mountain crest without seeing a sheep. It is a very broken country. There is no sweep of view along the mountains, and the sheep are mostly hidden to view. It is delightfully cool out of the sun all day, and quite hot in it. I never have worked harder and seen so few sheep. But tramping among the mountains and thinking of my wife and children is a joy.

Nov. 26. Another perfect day. I started early toward the north. All through the morning I tramped, up through a canyon exposed to the sun and over the range, and looked over on the other side, but saw nothing. Then I returned and climbed over a high pass, finding a big canyon below. It was noon and I went out of the canyon, intending to come back and hunt it in the p.m. I circled around the foot of the mountains and looked up canyons and saw nothing. A sheep trail runs on the desert close to the mountain.

I made a cup of tea and started back to the big canyon, reaching it about 3:15 p.m. Immediately I climbed the slope of a mountain at the foot of the canyon and looked over the country with my field glasses. Half a mile distant, on a rough mountainside, I saw four rams. At last, after all these days of such hard work, here was a chance for a fair stalk. I dropped down to a wash and, hidden by ironwood trees, I started up the canyon, having marked the spot where the rams were feeding on the mountain. It was a very steep mountain with the slope broken by precipices and small canyons. I walked with great caution, stepping noiselessly, and slowly when necessary, until reaching a previously selected point at the foot of a steep slope. I carefully started up the mountain slope and the excitement of the stalk was on. I was not in sight of the rams, but knew about where they were. Climbing small cliffs and, step by step, crawling up rocks, arranging footsteps so as not to make noise, I finally reached a level with the rams, and then began the approach up and down precipices and gullies along the slope. Slowly, slowly, bringing all my experience to bear, I kept approaching the spot. Finally I thought I was near, and emerging from a canyon I cautiously looked over.

No rams in sight. But a sudden sound of a falling rock and I knew the next gully crossed would bring them in sight a hundred yards off. Had they heard me? With strained excitement I descended the perpendicular side of the small canyon and climbed the opposite side, slowly so as to keep my breath, and paused before looking over. Another rock fell. I cocked the rifle, worked around on my back, and slowly rose in sitting posture, elbows on knees.

The largest ram was a hundred feet above the others, standing on a rock looking down over the country—a wonderful sight. The other three were feeding below. The side of the mountain seemed perpendicular, all broken. The surrounding jagged crestlines were tipped by sunlight, the sun having sunk below them. Below was the desert, with giant cactus studding the rich soil and the washes lined by ironwood trees.

One shot killed the big ram in his tracks. A second shot and another dropped. A third knocked over another. The other was

Charles Sheldon with a ram killed near Raven Butte at the north end of the Tinajas Altas Mountains. E. A. Goldman.

four years old—too small to shoot. The last two rams rose and started to stagger upward. A shot at each dropped them, one dead, the other with his hind legs broken so he could not move. The little ram stood a hundred feet above, looking down. It soon started upward and disappeared over the top. I hurried to each and photographed them, having to kill the last. It was almost dark. I gralloched [disemboweled] each, descended, and reached camp after dark. More about the sheep tomorrow.

Thus, after hard, cautious work, success comes. I found this morning that my sight was turned to 200 yards. This new sight thus gets out of order and it is quite possible that this is the reason I missed the ram day before yesterday. Proebstel is back with letters from Louisa. How I long to embrace her and how I love her! Tomorrow all will go for the meat and skins and I will get a rest from my hard tramping.

Nov. 27. Perfect day. At 3 a.m. the noise of approaching horses in camp alarmed us with the fear of being raided by Mexicans. Soon two men rode in, one exclaiming he had a telegram, and my heart sank. I grabbed it, lit a match, and found that my baby daughter was seriously sick. At daylight Murray was at once sent to find the horses, and I started with Goldman to show him the sheep on the mountain. Win drove the wagon around a black mountain and up the wash near the sheep.

After hastily photographing, I returned to camp and started for Wellton, riding mile after mile in the dark, reaching Wellton at 2 a.m. Then I sent a telegram to New York. A Thanksgiving dance was in full blast at Gale's with all the western vigor. Now I must wait to hear definitely from Louisa.

The rams were fine ones—one old, about seven years, the others five years. All were very dark with some summer hair not yet shed. They had been in the wash feeding on ironwood and palo verde and their stomachs contained other weeds not yet identified. But ironwood leaves seem to be the principal food. There was no fat on or in them. Their necks are slender. The black mountain [Raven Butte] near which I killed them is covered with broken lava and has a flat top.

The Gila Mountains [Tinajas Altas Mountains] are more broken than any mountain range I have ever been in. They are from six hundred to 2,000 feet above the plain, the back peaks probably 2,500 feet and some 3,000 feet. They are one mass of irregular, ragged crests and canyons with side canyons, and every hundred yards small canyons branching off from the side canyons. All the mountain slopes are exceedingly steep and seamed every hundred feet with gulches which make a continuous network of irregular spurs with almost perpendicular sides. Among these mountains it is impossible to see but a minute portion of the surface.

The ironwood and palo verde trees are mostly along the washes at the bottom of the principal canyons. Giant cactus are scattered about the surface, as are the hateful Bigelow chollas and now and then a bisnaga. The agave and a species of yucca appear scattered about the higher reaches, as well as some palo verde.

Hummingbirds buzz about the canyons and phainopeplas are ever present. Say's flycatchers [Say's phoebes] are always present with a sweet note in the canyons. Little lizards are often seen. Higher among the upper canyons, and even lower among the rocks, antelope spermophiles [ground squirrels] are common. The nests of pack rats are everywhere. A coyote made music about the camp last night but did not come into the traps. This morning I saw a flock of Gambel's quail, also a jack rabbit while riding in the p.m. Jacks are not very abundant. Desert foxes are about. I see some spiders, and brown butterflies are flitting about all the washes and canyons. The note of the rock wren is the common one about the mountains. The canyon wren does not sing although they are common.

The most surprising thing is the mosquitoes which, with a buzz more like that of a fly, continually attack us at night. The nights have been sharp but only chilly, not cold. It is hot during the day in the sun, but always cool in the shadow. Cottontail rabbits are here and I saw one this morning. Bird life is not abundant — I cannot recognize all of them. I have seen no golden eagles in the Gilas. The only enemies of sheep are the ever-abundant coyotes, a rare mountain lion, and perhaps bobcats, although Win says they are not in the southern desert ranges.

I am daily beholding all the glory of the desert coloration, now from the mountain tops, now from the slopes, and again from vistas through the canyons. The evening sunsets are beautiful, and at night the brilliant sky reminds me of my life in Mexico. This desert is not like the Chihuahua deserts. There the only cactus are *Opuntias* [cholla and prickly pear], and creosote and a few other herbs cover the ground — most of it is pebbly earth. Here I see the giant cactus, two kinds of cholla, two species of *Echinocereus* [hedgehog cactus], bisnagas, a species of prickly pear (rare and high up), and one or two other rare species about. Ironwoods and palo verdes are common in the washes, together with *Encelia* about the surface. In local patches the galleta grass is common. This desert is certainly among the most arid regions of America, but it teems with life. The sands in the washes show the tracks of the small animals. I am getting in better condition daily.

Grave of a man, woman, and their two children, who died of thirst eight miles east of Tinajas Altos. Charles Sheldon.

Nov. 28. Perfect day, then windy and disagreeable. Killing time all day—I am terribly worried and waiting for a telegram.

Nov. 29. Perfect day. At 2 p.m. I received a telegram from Louisa urging me to go back to camp—my daughter is recovering. I took the long ride and arrived at Raven Tank in the Gilas.

Nov. 30. Very windy, disagreeable. We packed up in the morning and rode to Tinajas Altas, and after lunching rode 8 miles out on the desert and made camp in the dark. I saw a red-tailed hawk, Bendire's thrasher, and a cottontail. The Pinacate Mountains were clear in the distance, and also a high range in lower California. The colors in the desert were exquisite.

Dec. 1. A light frost last night for the first time. We left the camp in the desert and approached the Tule Mountains. Two grave sites were seen on the desert—one where a man and wife and two children perished from thirst while bisnaga cactus was all around and Tinajas Altas was only eight miles away. The Cabeza Prieta range was on the left with the peak showing plainly. The desert has changed somewhat, there being large fields of a small cholla cactus around [Devil cholla]. We saw a shrike.

Camp among the ironwoods. Left to right, Charles Sheldon, Win Proebstel, and Murray Chappel. E. A. Goldman.

A saguaro cactus girdled by bighorn sheep. Charles Sheldon.

We reached Tule Tank at noon, 20 miles from Tinajas Altas, and found it dry. After taking lunch, we pulled through the range 3 miles more to Tule Well, a hundred years old, the ruins of an adobe house nearby. As usual, Goldman and I rode. The view of the Tule Mountains toward the Mexican line was seen through a vista of peaks and was particularly fine. We are camped among the ridges, the Pinta range in sight to the east. I did not mention that all the rams had ticks in their ears.

Dec. 2. Hard frost at night, windy, clear. Win and I left early in the a.m. and rode three miles to the mountains. I left him and hunted all day afoot. The north end of these Tule Mountains is different from the Gilas—the formation is somewhat different, much lava on the west part, and the mountains are a complex mass extending north and south for 20 miles, with a wide valley between the ranges. The crestline is smoother, and in general so are the slopes. But all the slopes are rocky, bone dry, and steep. There are not as many caves—the rocks seem to have resisted erosion better.

All day I tramped up slopes and canyons and saw only old sheep sign. It has been dry so long that even the ironwood leaves are white and the sheep seem to have left this locality. This is a great disappointment. I saw a golden-crowned kinglet, a jack rabbit, and the usual birds. Late at night I reached camp after an interesting though barren day. Win had ridden 10 miles down along the east slopes and had seen no fresh sign.

Dec. 3. Hard frost, perfect day. Win and I started riding around the mountains for 25 miles to make a reconnaissance for sheep sign. While going around, I saw numerous sahuaro cactus which had been chewed by the sheep for four or five feet above the ground. Some of them were 200 yards from the foot of the mountain. One sees these chewed sahuaros everywhere among the mountains and near them. This is the way the sheep get water when necessary. We saw a few fresh tracks at the corner of one mountain to the east. Then we passed through a canyon and took the mules down a very steep boulder slope and found a few more fresh signs. I climbed a mountain and went along the crest but saw nothing.

We rode several miles south down in Mexico but there the country was so dry that no sheep sign appeared. It seems that in the desert where rains are strictly local the sheep move to points where there has been rain. Rain makes the ironwood leaves green and nutritious, and also all the other vegetation. These sheep do not keep to chosen spots, except near water in summer. I saw three red-tailed hawks, a pack rat nest of cholla, and an antelope squirrel right under a peak, also the common ants' nests. We saw a border monument marking the boundary, the old boundary survey road and a camp still plain after 20 years. It looks very doubtful for sheep as we have the misfortune to be at a point of long drought. We reached camp at dark.

Dec. 4. Frost, perfect day. I started early, went along the extreme outside range, but saw no sign. Then I crossed the desert to the base of the main range and made tea. I went into a large basin and hunted many canyons, climbed one and wandered about the crest, descended the other side of the mountain, but saw no fresh sign of sheep all day. I had started ahead of the others with a horse, which I had tied in a canyon. I reached the horse at dark and found camp, which had been moved against the base of the mountain ½ mile north of the boundary line and 2 miles south of Tule Tanks. It is warmer here than at the last camp.

Dec. 5. Frost, perfect day. I started early and climbed a high mountain and circled the whole crest without seeing fresh sign. Old beds were everywhere along the crest above and halfway down the spurs. I descended and made tea, and then ascended to boundary monument 185. This gave me a chance, by looking at the monuments on both sides, to locate the line. I saw a shrike. This is a very high mountain and I kept on and circled the crests all the afternoon.

At four I started to descend a spur, very steep, and when a third of the way down saw a single fair-sized ewe standing along the crest of the spur, looking at me. I judged it 300 yards and my bullet struck 2 feet under her. I fired three more times as she ran

Sheldon's rifle leans against boundary monument 185, high in the Tule Mountains. Charles Sheldon.

down the mountain but missed all. She crossed a wash and ascended another mountain. I descended and, although the sun was setting, followed her and reached the crest of the mountain at dark without seeing her. Then I cut an agave staff and descended over the steep slope and down a canyon and finally

It is on incredibly rough peaks like this one in the Tule Mountains that bighorn sheep are found. Boundary monument 186 sits near the top of this peak. E. A. Goldman.

walked, or rather stumbled, around the base of the mountains to camp. Win had ridden to the south end of the mountains and reports fresh feed. He killed a two-year-old ram. Tomorrow I shall go there and camp alone.

Dec. 6. Frost, perfect day. Early in the a.m. Win and I started riding, leading a pack mule with my robe, provisions, and 10 gallons of water in desert water bags. We came across the line directly south, about eight miles, to within 2 miles of the sand belt which extends around a vast circle and flanks the lava of Pinacate. We arrived here in the Tuseral Mountains about 10 a.m., then Win left with the horses, leaving me alone. I made my camp under a palo verde tree by simply stretching out my robe and bringing some rocks for handy things to place articles on. I have two lard buckets, tea, sugar, oatmeal, rice, salt, and some bread. We forgot the frying pan.

After taking some tea, I started south, went up a basin and canyon and climbed to the top of the mountain. The vast sand belt stretched around before me with the Pinacate Mountains and the black lava-cone country just beyond. The Tuseral Mountains are also a complex mass, with high, jagged peaks and deep canyons between numerous knife-edged spurs. They are just as much broken as are all these desert mountains. But the whole desert vegetation about here is fresh and green, the iron-wood trees, the mesquite (rare), palo verde, and acacias. The *Encelia* blooms richly with its bright daisylike yellow flowers. Some of the galleta grass is green and the *Encelia* leaves are rich sage green and full and lovely.

The giant cactus is all about but the hateful Bigelow cholla is absent, except a rare plant high in the mountains. All cactus here is scarce. The valleys between the mountain ranges are wide and rich with vegetation. Sheep sign is everywhere and the washes are full of their tracks.

I kept ascending and descending the spurs high up under the crest but saw nothing but sheep beds everywhere in the saddles. Then I descended over the cliffy ground on the north side of the mountain and followed the wash to a beautiful canyon between high ranges and encircled by rough and fantastic peaks at the head. It was nearly dark, and looking up on the crestline my eye caught an animal. My glasses revealed a ewe, standing, apparently looking at me. Then more to the right, in a separate band, a three-year-old ram and two smaller ones, all looking, as sheep do. They, after a careful looking-over of the country below, passed over the crest to lie down. But the ewe stood and watched me. Then as I left I saw her lie down against a rock on the crest.

My trouble in this hunting is too many people, too much riding around by Win, etc. I reached camp after dark. A high wind came up and after cooking rice I went under my robe.

Dec. 7. Warm night, perfect day. The wind blew a hurricane all night, but I slept through, with periods of awakening and looking at my watch to note the time. At 5:30 I was up, a fire started, some oatmeal cooking. I waited until 7 a.m., when I could just see the sights of my rifle, and started. The wind had slackened, and I went cautiously in the dim light along the wash at the base of this mountain and then crossed over into the canyon I was in late yesterday afternoon. Slowly I walked up through it, climbing points and looking about with great caution, but saw nothing. When I reached the head I saw trails leading up to the narrow canyon that leads up into an amphitheater of mountains, broken with canyons and surrounded by a network of them, with cliffs and pinnacles shooting up all around. Numerous sheep had traveled up, and also coyotes and other small animals.

Excited by the idea of finding water, I hurried up and finally discovered a fine tank 15 feet long and five feet wide, narrowing at the ends. It was filled with sand, but there was a three-foot circle of open water back in a cave. I probed with a stick and it went down ten feet or more but did not hit the end. This is a great discovery! It is a larger tinaja than Tule Tank. Horses can be brought within 100 feet of it. There is 25 feet of almost perpendicular rock below the tank, but it is easy to climb. Mosquito wigglers were in the water. Some sheep had drunk of it, and several flocks of small birds were about—unknown to me. It is possible that other water might be found by digging in some of the dry tinajas.

I took a long drink and went half a mile up the canyon. Then I descended, working my way down small perpendiculars, walled in by cliffs with the peaks shooting up about me. The vista down the canyon revealed the encircling ranges and bright green of the ironwoods and other vegetation. As I emerged I sat down and looked about with my field glasses. About halfway up a very steep mountain cut with gorges and canyons and rising to a sharp, wonderful peak, I saw a big, old ram slowly ascending and working about among the ironwoods.

At once I selected a route and started climbing along the steep side, ascending and descending the gorges and canyons, using all the caution taught by my experience. As I neared the point, a deep gorge caused me to ascend still higher so as to get across it. Slinging my rifle, I worked down a dangerous cliff, then up the bottom, and at last the final climb up a wall of rock 50 feet high. At the top I knew I would either see the ram within shot or find that he had run away. I had once heard a rock fall above. I had not seen him after starting—I had carefully picked a

The Tuseral Mountains in Sonora, with lush Sonoran Desert vegetation in foreground. Charles Sheldon bagged a big ram on the high peak in the background. Charles Sheldon.

route out of sight. Step by step I worked up the cliff and at last paused to get my breath before I emerged on top. Then, working over on my stomach, I saw the ram 150 yards above, slowly ascending an almost perpendicular wall, not suspecting me. It was ten a.m.

My first bullet misfired! I fired offhand at his hind quarters, my only chance. The bullet struck. He turned and ran down awkwardly with a broken hind leg. He looked big with fine horns as the sun shone on him. As he reached the edge of a canyon I fired again and the bullet struck him so that he pitched sideways and the momentum sent him down the steep, almost perpendicular rocks for a hundred yards, then he disappeared in an arroyo. I knew he was mine. I hastened down and found him dead. A veteran old ram, scabby with hair almost gone, front knees bare and calloused, one horn badly broken in the middle from butting, the skin on his face scarred from fighting. His ears were full of ticks and almost stopped up. He was in exceedingly ragged condition and had had hard fighting. It was a romantic spot to kill an old ram.

Then the photographing. I dragged him to a favorable spot for measuring and took off the skin as the sun beat down. In two hours it was off. He had eaten almost exclusively ironwood leaves. Then I cut off a hind leg, put it and the skin in my rucksack, shouldered the head, and tramped under the hot sun to camp, reaching it at 2 p.m. Then a cup of tea.

After salting the skin I started south, working among the canyons to the sand belt, and returned to camp after dark without seeing another sheep. I saw four quail fly out of an ironwood tree at dusk.

Then a cup of tea, a bit of bread, and after putting a pail of meat on to boil, I write these notes. The moon is two-thirds full, the desert is absolutely silent. Peaks and ranges surround me. The moonlight streams down through the palo verde tree on my little camp. The air is scarcely chilly. The sky is absolutely clear and the stars shine and twinkle through the moonlight. Not even an insect makes a sound. I am thinking with love of my dear sweet wife and children.

Dec. 8. Perfect day. I started before daylight, after getting up several times in the night to keep the mutton boiling so that I could have a pot of soup. I had made up my mind to hunt especially for ewes and secure at least two for the Biological Survey — they particularly wanted ewes. The ewes stay back high in the mountains and this is the first country I have ever hunted sheep where ewes are more difficult to find and kill than rams.

I passed alongside the mountain near camp, carefully watching the slopes and canyons, but saw nothing. Going around the end, I crossed 2 miles of desert to a rugged range bordering the sand belt. Then I climbed through a canyon to the crest, a very rugged and dangerous crest to climb along. I surmounted several extremely dangerous peaks and went along the crests of knife-edged spurs, always carefully watching the broken rock country below. At times the views were magnificent, looking over the great sand belt and across the black lava country to Pinacate rising in the distance, with scattered volcanic cones lifting up about the rolling country. At times I could get glimpses of the Gulf of California, although a haze usually hung over it.

At about 11 a.m. I spotted three ewes feeding about the slope of a spur within shot from the crest. But I had a difficult and dangerous time to proceed along it to within shot. Only one ewe was large enough to shoot, the others were two-year-olds. It required an hour of dangerous work to come within shot, but at last I had them 125 yards below me, all standing, looking down. It was a fine sensation to sit and take aim from the crest, with the wonderful views surrounding me and the fine sight of the wild sheep standing on the rim of the rocky spur. I pulled the trigger and a misfire! Then a second and a third misfire! The fourth pull of the trigger brought the report and the ewe staggered and soon rolled down and down and caught in the rocks about halfway to the bottom of the canyon. One of the smaller ewes soon disappeared, but the other stood looking at the dead ewe below. I cannot forget the descent over the cliffs and boulders and rocky crags, but I accomplished it. The little ewe soon appeared in the rocks a hundred yards above and watched me. After photographing, I measured her and took off her skin. Then I made tea and cooked some of her liver on the coals. Soon, across the canyon on the rim of a spur, I saw a three-year-old ram and two yearlings, all standing, looking on the other side. They passed over without having seen me. I had heard rocks falling opposite me, and although not 200 yards away, I looked again and again with glasses, but the slopes are so broken that I did not see these sheep. I found great quantities of acacia in the ewe's stomach, some palo verde, but no ironwood. I cut off her hindquarters and prepared to depart.

I descended through the canyon, my feet giving me excruciating pain under the load as my shoes, having filled with sand, had badly blistered them. Reaching the plain, I put the meat, head, and skin on a rock and proceeded along the mountain to the sand belt but saw nothing. Then I returned, picked up the load, and reached camp at dark to find Win there with a new supply of water. He will spend the night. The wind roars but it is not cold.

Dec. 9. Windy in the a.m., perfect in p.m. All night the wind seemed to blow in a quantity of mosquitoes which kept directing their course toward my face. At daylight I started as Win was saddling to go back to the other camp. Last night I sewed patches on my trousers for the fourth time and also patched my moccasins. Blisters had opened on the bottom of my feet and they were badly crippled. I struggled along to warm them up, but all day they have been very painful.

I started up a big canyon to the north and gradually worked toward the head. My feet were so sore, and I had to watch my steps so carefully among the rocks, that I failed to see a fairly good ram high on the slope at the head of the canyon until he ran. He then went out of sight before I could get a shot. Then I climbed to the crest—not as dangerous a climb as yesterday, but the crests about this canyon were equally as bad and the spurs worse. The mountains about this basin are exceedingly rugged and imposing.

I kept limping along the cliffs and around the pinnacles until 1:30 p.m. when I sighted two ewes on the pinnacle of a spur not far below and within a 200-yard shot, one small, the other fair. A shot killed the larger one, which rolled about 50 feet down and caught on a very steep slope. Then I was surprised to see another small ewe, still lying on a rock nearby, apparently undisturbed by the rifle shot. At last I had accomplished my task to kill two ewes, and a difficult one it has been. It required a great deal of experience to go back on the crests and find them without disturbing them before a shot.

It was too steep to measure her. I made tea under a cliff in a romantic spot where I found a palo verde tree with dead limbs. I only had a shelf two feet wide for a fire, but the view along the summit, with the line of peaks and the mountain ranges about, was inspiring. It was clear and calm and I felt all the romance of my location. The raven, my constant companion in sheep hunting north and south, flew about, waiting for its feast. Her stomach contained the same material as the other ewe—no ironwood.

I skinned the ewe, packed it with the head in my rucksack, and murdered my feet climbing down and going through the rocky canyon to the plain. I reached camp at dark, just limping.

I am again alone, an outlaw in Mexico near the route of the *insurrectos*. The moon shines nearly full, the mountains about are mystical. The wind is beginning to roar.

Dec. 10. Windy night, perfect day. I looked at my watch and saw by moonlight what I thought was 5:30 and got up, made a fire, cooked and ate breakfast, and waited for daylight. But after half an hour, when it didn't get lighter, I looked at my watch and what was my disgust to find that it was only 3:15 a.m.! Back under the robe, I slept until six, then took a cup of tea and started.

I hunted a long canyon beyond the others to the north, climbing many spurs and to the crest once. I saw a three-year-old ram and a yearling within easy killing distance but did not disturb them. After lunch I went up the canyon where I killed the big ram, hoping to find something near the water. I was surprised to see a golden eagle eating the carcass while several ravens flew about, squawking. Seeing no sheep, I came back and hunted along the north side of the mountain near camp, but saw nothing and reached camp at dark.

The moonlight on the desert is brilliant and strange. There is not even a sound of an insect. It is calm, only the light crackle of a small fire greets the ears. Only two days more of hunting! But I have my sheep and now think of nothing but my lovely wife and children.

Dec. 11. Perfect day. Last night about nine, when I was asleep, I was aroused by the tramping of horses, and looking out saw three horses and two riders in front of me. As the thought of Mexicans came over me, I heard Win's voice. He and Goldman had been in the sand belt to set traps. They gave me letters from Louisa telling about my dear little daughter. How eagerly I read them and what a feeling of love they produced. Soon I will be speeding to her.

Early in the morning I left to hunt a northern canyon as Win and Goldman were packing to go back to their camp. I tramped to the head of the canyon and on to the crest but saw nothing. In the afternoon I hunted the side canyons. In one I

Rodents in traps—a long day of specimen preparation ahead. E. A. Goldman.

saw a three-year-old ram and a yearling within easy shot. In another, another three-year-old ram, and in another yet another three year old. I did not molest them. Finally I went up a long canyon winding far back in rugged ranges, lured on by the numerous sheep tracks indicating water. Far up near the head I found five tinajas containing all together about 100 gallons of water, but these will be dry in a month or two. I went too far and darkness overtook me, but the moonlight was enough and it seemed strange and lovely to pick out a light-strewn path down the canyon, enclosed by the rocky walls and slopes of the mountains. After emerging I tramped two miles across the desert, lonely, lonely, but impressive. Then a fire, some cooked meat, and my cup of tea. My thoughts are of loved ones at home.

Dec. 12. Cloudy, but a fine day. By moonlight I left camp, walked a mile and a half north, and hunted the canyons all day, twice clambering along the crests. At two different times I saw rams—one three years old, the other four years old, both within easy shot. I did not disturb them. I noticed where one ram had come up to Win's horse's tracks and had jumped back on reaching them, then started to run along them, and then off on the mountain without crossing them. A mile above here the cholla belt is reached. Why it should end there I cannot say.

Sheep are very abundant in this part of the mountains, but they are not in bands—singles, twos, threes, and fours perhaps, sometimes fives. They are separated and haunt the broken parts of the mountains, the ewes highest up as a rule. It is most difficult to find them and it does little good to look with glasses, such a small fraction of the surface is visible. It means tramp, tramp, tramp, climb and descend, until they are in sight or started and run.

This is my last night here alone. Tomorrow Win comes with the horses and then I go as straight and fast as possible to my dear wife and children. But I cannot forget these mystic nights, sitting alone here in camp in the moonlit desert—the calm, the silence, the radiance of the mountains, the softness of the light, and the mystery pervading the scene. My trip has been completely successful and now I have the thought of going back to home and dear ones. The sunsets have been wonderful, especially tonight with the lighted clouds changing from golden to crimson to pink, all seen through vistas of the craggy mountain masses. As I look out on the desert in moonlight, it seems so soft and hospitable—the sense of its death-dealing aridity is lost. I shall hunt for an hour at daylight in the morning. This will be my last. Then all my thoughts will be centered on home.

Dec. 13. Perfect day. Mosquitoes were frequent all night. I started by moonlight and in two hours completely circled the mountain near camp without seeing a sheep or fresh sign made since I first went about it. I shot a female cottontail rabbit for Goldman. The variety of green on the desert is impressive. The ironwoods are a deep green to a light green, according to the conditions and moisture received. The mesquite is a pure, unvarying green. The palo verde a pea green, lighter in shade. The *Encelia* is even lighter than a sage green. Other composites have varying shades, from sage green to light greens. The creo-

Lunch at Tinajas Altas. Left to right: Win Proebstel, Murray Chappel, and Charles Sheldon. E. A. Goldman.

sote bush, the most abundant shrub, has the deepest green. And also, on the mountainsides, are the *Elaphrium*. I have taken my last hunt.

At about 10 a.m. Win came with the horses. We packed and reached the camp in two hours. The night when Win and Goldman came to my camp I had thought I had heard shots. This was true. Murray had heard four shots. Later, tracks showed that a Mexican had struck our trail and followed it toward the line, and then turned back. Also, another Mexican's fresh horse tracks showed below my camp. What were these Mexicans doing?

As we pulled out of camp with the team, Goldman and I rode ahead to visit some traps he had set and found a coyote in one, which I photographed. We pulled on until just at the edge of the mountains and made camp.

Dec. 14. Cloudy, no sun. We left early, rode across the desert, and reached Tinajas Altas at 1:30 when we lunched and took water. The tracks of several Mexicans, 8 to 12, showed they had been there since we last passed. Then we went on the main road until dark and made camp. Win took one of the horses with a pack saddle and went to our old camp at the black mountain for the rams' heads and meat, but found that the coyotes had reached and eaten nearly all the meat.

Dec. 15. Perfect day. Left early and reached Wellton without incident at 2:30. Then hustled and took the Sunset Limited train for New York at 5:30, only to find that floods near Houston would probably delay us 24 or more hours. Thus ends this delightful trip.

Aerial view of the Pinacate country in northwestern Sonora. Sierra Hornaday in fore-ground, MacDougal Crater center right, Sierra Pinacate in the background. Peter L. Kresan.

3

IN THE PINACATE COUNTRY, SONORA, 1915

This trip takes Charles Sheldon southward from his earlier camp in the Tule Mountains to search for sheep in the lava and desert landscapes of Mexico's Sierra Pinacate and Sierra Blanca. Win Proebstel has again been hired to assist him along with another local man, Staley Hovatter. As during his previous trip, the Mexican Revolution was still in progress.

Unlike his previous visit to the Sonoran Desert, this trip was made during an unusually rainy period. Sheldon finds the desert floor transformed into a carpet of pink sand verbenas, yellow and white evening primroses, and other showy wildflowers. Weather records disclose that during the preceding month, January 1915, 2.56 inches of rain fell at nearby Yuma, Arizona. This is the second wettest January on record for this station.

The first non-Indian to explore the Sierra Pinacate was the far-ranging Father Eusebio Kino. The tireless Jesuit missionary made several expeditions into the lava fields of the extinct volcano, and climbed its summit twice, in 1698 and again in 1706. From the summit of what he named Cerro Santa Clara, he could see the head of the Gulf of California with his spyglass and confirmed that Baja California was not an island.

Nor was Sheldon the first American hunter to seek mountain sheep in the Pinacate lava and in the Sierra Blanca. In the fall of 1907, Dr. William T. Hornaday, director of the New York Zoological Park, Dr. Daniel T. MacDougal, John M. Phillips, and Godfrey Sykes climbed 3,960-foot Pinacate Peak and collected several mountain sheep and pronghorn antelope in the region. The exploits of this expedition were described in Hornaday's book Campfires on Desert and Lava, *published in 1908, and in a 1908 article by MacDougal, "Across Papagueria." Many of the geographical names mentioned by Sheldon, such as Hornaday Mountains, MacDougal Crater, Sykes Crater, Phillips Butte, and Rainbow Ridge, are from Hornaday's book and an accompanying map prepared by Sykes. These names do not appear on modern Mexican maps.*

In the winter of 1909–1910, explorer-ethnologist Carl Lumholtz visited the Sierra Pinacate and Sierra Blanca, where his guides shot both sheep and antelope. Lumholtz published the results of his expedition in his book New Trails in Mexico *(1912), and his detailed map of the region was the best available to Sheldon. By the time of Sheldon's arrival, prospectors had also visited the Sierra Pinacate, as indicated by notes found by Sheldon dated March 1914. The notes were left by Dr. Louis D. Ricketts and John C. Greenway. Ricketts was a well-known mining engineer, and Greenway, a friend of Theodore Roosevelt and a member of the Rough Riders in the Spanish-American War, was the developer of the large New Cornelia copper mine at Ajo, Arizona. They were guided by Reuben Daniels, one of the colorful Southwest desert characters of the early 1900s. Daniels had accompanied the Hornaday expedition to the Sierra Pinacate as a guide in 1907 before being sent back for shooting at everything in sight. His name lives on as Daniels Arroyo south of Ajo.*

Sheldon observed long-abandoned Indian camps near the water holes in the Pinacate Country. These had been occupied either by a historic group of nomads called Sand Papagos or Areneños, or by the prehistoric people known to archaeologists as the Amaragosa Culture. The Sand Papagos, never numerous, had disappeared by the time of Sheldon's visit.

Feb. 6, 1915, Saturday. We started from Wellton, Arizona, at three p.m., Win Proebstel, Staley Hovatter, and myself, with three mules and four horses. Thursday I had been to Mexicali and had obtained a letter from General Cantú, military dictator of lower California, giving me a pass to the Pinacate region, with which he has nothing to do. After driving for 5½ hours across the desert, we reached Win's camp at Copper Mountain. Our wagon was drawn by two mules.

There have been recent heavy rains—the desert was much greener than a year ago. Ocotillo was leafed out and *Encelia* was in bloom, though not very plentifully near Wellton. A pink flower now was scattered over the desert, also a yellow one and a white one. It was a beautiful day, warm and balmy. I rode along, happy in observing all the familiar points of the Gila range, recalling my experiences of a year ago. Toward evening the sky to the west and south was banded by ribbons of pink and

Wildflowers near the Sierra Tuseral in Sonora. Charles Sheldon.

crimson clouds in parallel layers stretching clear around that part of the horizon. Few birds were observed. Now and then a coyote track was seen, or those of stray cattle, which at this season feed far out on the desert. I slept under a brilliant sky.

Feb. 7. Perfect day. We traveled for eight hours to Tule Tanks. Much of the ocotillo is in bloom. Also, a great variety of weeds coming up gives the desert a greenish floor. It was hot during the middle hours of the day. After going to the end of the Buck Mountains, we turned to the left (east) and wound along the base of the Cabeza Prieta range and passed between the ranges on a flat, narrow desert to the Tule Tanks. Many flowers are blooming and I collected several. Coyote tracks are abundant everywhere, much more so than a year ago. I saw a jack rabbit. Also, we saw the tracks of two small whitetail deer on the desert—Win has observed them here for three years. He says sheep feed much on palo verde in May and June. Birds were more abundant. I saw a phainopepla, a mockingbird, and rock wrens. I noticed several sheep tracks, one along the Cabeza

The packtrain heads into the sand belt north of the Pinacate lava field. Charles Sheldon.

Prietas, more along the Tule Mountains. The Cabeza Prietas practically join the Tules. We have Win's same horses and mules as last year, an extra mule, and a horse of Staley's, which I ride. Although tired and sore, I enjoyed the ride in this glorious desert. *Encelia* was brilliantly in bloom in places. There was a heavy dew in the night.

Feb. 8. Perfect day. In 3½ hours we came to my old lone camp in the Tuseral Mountains. The desert was wonderful in its blooms. I collected many flowers of many different colors. The blooming *Encelia* covers everything and even grows high on the mountains. This causes the giant cactus to look drab. I saw many birds, a cottontail, and a jack rabbit.

After lunching, I took my rifle and went up the valley to Sheldon Tank and far above it, near the mountain crests. Not a sign of a sheep did I see, not even a track. At about 5:30 I saw a big ewe high above on the crestline. I thought she was heavy with lamb. This was way back, up high in the interior, and this ewe was overly cautious. I reached camp after dark.

A "tree" cholla (chain-fruit cholla) stands alone in the sand. Charles Sheldon.

Hummingbirds are very abundant, even high on the mountains. Little lizards are running about. The desert floor is mostly green. I can never forget this day of riding among the flowers. I am sore but "coming in" [to shape]. Owls kept hooting last night.

Feb. 9. A few clouds, a faint breeze. We traveled for 1 hour and 50 minutes to the sand, and 2 hours and 20 minutes across it. Then we failed to get on the trail and traveled eastward the whole length of Hornaday Mountain. We lunched and I got out the maps. We turned back and in less than 3 hours reached the Papago Tanks, well described by Hornaday and Lumholtz. Five or six tanks are full of water and the arroyo bed above has much water. Within two miles of the sand the organ pipe cactus begins.

The feature of the day was the blooms on the sand, particularly toward the north side. One carpet of flowers—a yellow daisylike flower, large white flowers, pink flowers, and others—a thickly bedded flower garden. There is less vegetation on the lava. Coyote tracks are everywhere. The sand belt is fairly green after the rains. It is full of gopher and kangaroo rat holes, so much so that travel is difficult. A short distance north of the sand the tree cholla begins and it is scattered over the sand belt. Sheep tracks were fairly abundant on the flat close to the south end of the Tule Mountains, but none were feeding on iron-woods. Tomorrow I take my first hunt, without much chance of getting anything.

Feb. 10. Fair, a cool breeze. I left at daylight for Sykes Crater and reached there in less than an hour. A coyote almost came in camp just before I left. I saw an old sheep track in the lava about 1/2 mile from the crater. I watched Sykes Crater for an hour but saw no sheep. Then I ascended Phillips Butte, directly west of the crater by my compass, and saw nothing but some very old sheep tracks and dung. Another small, shallow crater to the west of Phillips Butte had some water in it. I returned to Sykes Crater and descended to the bottom from the west side. A few old sheep tracks were on the slopes and a very few old tracks in the bottom. Tree chollas, Bigelow chollas, palo verdes, iron-woods, greasewood, *Encelia,* a snap-dragon flower, and a few others were abundant. *Elaphrium microphyllum* was on the slopes. I found an old red handkerchief like those of the Mexican revolutionists who I met a year ago—they may have hunted sheep in this crater. I ascended on the north side. I noted three other places where an ascent could be made—all are comparatively easy.

Then I went along the Rainbow Ridge, but saw only limited, old sheep sign. It is now clear that but few sheep are ever here, and there are none at this time. I noticed horse tracks going around the rim of the crater. My barometer made Phillips Butte 800 feet above Papago tanks, and Sykes Crater 750 feet from top to bottom. There is a peak 50 feet higher rising directly from the east side of the rim of the crater. Pack rats' nests of cholla were abundant on Phillips Butte and all along down the slopes of the crater. I noticed a cactus wren's nest in a cholla at the bottom. I also heard the wrens, and rock and canyon wrens and several other birds.

Papago Tanks gorge in flood. Charles Sheldon.

I reached camp after dark, having seen old sheep tracks out on the lava. I am inclined to think that sheep come here only at times, and then but very few. I do not see much small mammal sign in the lava. The view from the top of Phillips Butte is very fine in all directions—I took lunch on the top. I saw two antelope tracks today. *Encelia* was flowering all over the inside of Sykes Crater, both high and low. Win went looking for the horses, which strayed 4 miles north in the night.

Feb. 11. At daylight a rain came on which immediately developed into a severe storm with heavy squalls and downpours. Not prepared for rain, we all got soaked and stood about until the p.m. when it cleared. The volume of water which soon began to pour through the Papago gorge and tanks was tremendous, and one can realize how the tanks are made after seeing it. The other washes were flooded also. It has been a trying day and all have been very cold. After writing, about 6 p.m., a tremendous rain, and heavy hail at times, suddenly descended and everything, including ourselves, got soaked again.

Feb. 12. Perfect day. The gorge of the Papago Tanks is very long, extending through the country along the north side of the Pinacate range. It roared all night, and when we left in the morning was still running heavily. This is how the sand-loaded water cuts tanks. Tanks are more likely to be found in these very long river courses running from the high mountains.

The Sykes Crater, Rainbow Ridge, etc., are the direct extension of ridges running around in a semicircle from the main Pinacate range, and hence sheep wander out there. Owls keep hooting every night. Many birds are singing about, and the sweet notes of the Gambel sparrow [white-crowned sparrow] remind me of spring days in Alaska. The Costa hummingbird is abundant everywhere, even on the tops of the mountains. Ravens are plentiful, and coyotes howl every night. Jack rabbits and Gambel quails are abundant.

The night was clear and cold. We left about eleven, after drying everything, and took the old, well-defined trail directly south across the lava field, with the main range on the east and the sand belt on the west. The going was mostly good. We traveled for several hours toward the Tank of the Chivos. Apparently neither Lumholtz nor Hornaday knew of this trail. The day was without a breath of wind, without a cloud, and the sun just took the chill off the air. I have never ridden in more perfect weather. The lava, although scattered generally, in places seems to have been thrown off very thick in straight lines extending several miles. These belts are composed of very heavy rock in irregular masses and are, in places, hard to cross. We saw no antelope or tracks. Water was in all the arroyos.

About 4 p.m., after we had lunched and were continuing along at the foot of a small, isolated mountain just west of the Tank of the Chivos, I saw a ewe sheep run up over the top. I went up and shortly reached the spot, but the ewe had evidently run off—I don't know where. I saw a gray fox as I was looking for the ewe.

We camped at the foot of the south side of the mountain. The night was clear. The sunset, a band of deep crimson, circled the western horizon. The stars were brilliant as I lay in the robe, looking at the heavens and thinking of my dear wife and little ones. The coyotes were yelling all about us.

Feb. 13. Perfect weather. Win and I traveled with the horses and two pack mules for three hours to within 2 miles of Pinacate Peak. I decided to camp alone against the side of a canyon among very rough lava. I will make my fire against the wall of the canyon, out of sight of the mountains, and will sleep in a smoother place 50 yards away.

After a bite to eat, I started at 3:30 and went N.E. across the lava field. Tracks of sheep are scattered about the lava. Soon, two fair-sized rams came into the field of my glasses, feeding on the side of a low mountain slope. I planned a stalk, and circled around above them after they had passed out of sight around the slope. The difficulty of hunting here is that most of the lava rock, large and small, is loose on the ground so that one makes noise and has to watch the ground with the utmost caution and go very slowly.

I finally came up on top and paused to take breath, thinking the rams were within easy shot below. Then, looking over, I beheld cliffs and broken slopes and saw the rams 400 yards away, walking out on the lava. I chanced two shots and missed. I had made an excellent stalk, but the rams had gone in the wrong direction.

I can see the Gulf of California when I walk out from the canyon, but I am really encircled by the rocks in a wild spot. The chances seem good for sheep, but I must come back to camp before dark, since it would be a very dangerous undertaking to

Pinacate Peak (in background), a dormant volcano, as seen from the northwest. Charles Sheldon.

attempt to get there through broken, black lava fields in the dark—besides, it would be almost impossible to *find* the camp.

Feb 14. Perfect weather. I was off at daylight and have taken a long, old-time mountain tramp. First, I went up a peak two miles to the S.E. and there saw only old sheep sign. The steep slopes and cinders made climbing a little trying. Then I descended and went two miles toward the main range and saw two ewes about lunch time. After tea, I climbed to the crest where I had seen them, but could not find them. Then the rest of the afternoon I climbed up and down, completely circling the crests of the mountains this side of the main range. I saw ten sheep (9 ewes, one large ram) on the crest of the main range near Pinacate Peak, too far to go for them. The ram seemed to be herding and driving the ewes to a feeding place, where they fed for two or three hours.

All the sheep I have seen crop something close to the ground. The sheep outside the main range move restlessly, and while a stalk is being made they move off. There are few sheep tracks in the lava below the mountains, and on the outside ranges most of the sign is old. The main body of sheep seems to be on the main range, so I must move camp near enough to hunt it. The sheep are very conspicuous to the field glasses on the smooth slopes of this mountain. They are as cautious as any other sheep I have seen.

At 1,500 feet the Bigelow cholla begins and the slopes are covered with it. A feature of the day was the cholla nests of pack rats. I have passed 48, many on the crests. These are among the most remarkable things I have ever seen. Ravens are abundant and I saw a large flock of vultures about 10 a.m., circling above a crest. Birds are not as abundant as they are lower down, but the hummingbirds and the wrens are everywhere. I see a great many cast coverings of the 1,000-legged worm. More about the scenery, vegetation, and character of the mountains later. Some honey bees were abundant at the Papago Tanks.

Feb. 15 (Monday). Overcast. I left early for the main range, intending to try for that band of ewes and the ram. It would be something worthwhile to stalk and kill a ram among a band of watchful ewes. It required two hours to reach the foot of the range, walking over the loose lava. I saw the shell of a turtle not far from camp. It threatened rain. I intended to ascend to the point where I saw the band yesterday, hoping to find them near there. This was the sharp peak of a summit near Pinacate Peak and surrounded on all sides by cliffs. I slowly toiled upward through a canyon. I noticed that at about 2,100 feet a variety of *Opuntia* prickly pear first appeared.

At about 11:30 I was near a sharp rim that led up to the peak among jagged rocks. Looking over the rim, I saw a ewe feeding on a slope of the peak, 400 yards away. Then, rising upward, I saw the ram and four other ewes. I knew the rest were below and all too far to shoot. There was no approach from my position. I therefore waited and ate some lunch. The ram and several others lay down. At no time was there a "sentinel." I could look over a vast landscape to the west, and the Gulf and salt playas were clear, also the mountains beyond.

After an hour, all the sheep arose, one ram, 8 ewes, and only one lamb, and they slowly fed upward and climbed the peak and disappeared. Then I climbed upward, over the cliffs and rocks, very slowly and with the utmost caution. The wind seemed to blow directly from me to them. At last I was at a point where, by standing, I could see the whole peak. Rising slightly, I saw, not fifty yards away, the horns of two ewes. I heard others walking. I knew the ram was there—I had but to rise quickly and shoot him. I cocked the rifle, selected my footing, when suddenly, but fifteen yards away, a lamb loudly bleated and I saw the little fellow, perhaps three weeks or a month old, standing, looking at me. It had been lying down between two rocks. Immediately, a large ewe jumped on a point of rock shooting up from the cliffs. She looked at me as I held the rifle, about to rise, but before I could rise up, the ram jumped alongside of her, not fifty yards away. Both were outlined on the skyline of the peak, a wonderful sight. I aimed at the heart of the ram, pulled the trigger, and a *misfire!* As I pulled the bolt, both jumped over the cliff and all of the other ewes followed—they had all been at the edge. The lamb ran up a little way, and a ewe came back and stood on a rock—I would not shoot her. Then she jumped over toward the lamb and ran off to the side, and the lamb followed. This was her method of enticing it to follow her.

I ran to the edge and saw all the sheep running across a saddle at the foot of the cliffs, and soon all stood ¼ mile distant on the side of a slope and watched me. Then an old ewe led the way and single file they went up a distant mountain, the ram bringing up the rear. But as they climbed the mountain slope, the ram left the band and disappeared. The ram was about seven years old. All the sheep were very brown, in contrast to the dark coats of those I saw in November, 15 months ago. This band had been occupying that spot for a long time.

I remained on the peak and looked over the country but saw nothing, and at 3:30 started for camp. Pack rats' nests were everywhere. I reached camp just before dark and, as rain threatened, I moved everything across the arroyo and prepared to receive a possible soaking.

As I write these notes, it seems to me that this was the worst piece of luck in all my experience sheep hunting—a fine stalk successfully made and all spoiled by the misfire. What is the trouble with my rifle?

Feb. 16, Tuesday. Overcast. Long before daylight, raindrops began to fall and I got up, put everything under canvas, and built a big fire. It proved to be but a light shower—drops have fallen at times all day.

About 11:00 a.m. Win came with a pack mule. We packed and I led the way on foot, and in a couple of hours we reached this point within a half a mile of the main range—a beautiful spot with a wonderful outlook. I have a canvas stretched across the limbs of a palo verde tree beside a canyon, with a deep gorge below where there is abundant water. On my right is a high, rocky mountain. In front is the first mountain I climbed. On my left the tumbled-up lava, and I can look down over the lava field to the sand and Gulf.

At three I took the rifle, tramped south across the lava field, climbed a mountain near Pinacate, and returned at dark without seeing anything. I observed the tracks and dung of horses up in a canyon close to Pinacate. I notice that the Bigelow cholla grows most abundantly on the fine cinder slopes. This fine cinder must provide a good soil for its growth. I notice all about here the giant cactus eaten by sheep.

Win killed a small ewe and a yearling ram on a small outside mountain yesterday. Another ewe he saw had a lamb. It is quite evident that a sheep or two may be on any of the small mountains. Antelope squirrels are abundant in the rocks and lava

A young saguaro grows in the lava near the crest of Pinacate Peak. Charles Sheldon.

everywhere. There is a wonderful sunset sky tonight. Mosquitoes swarm, and last night kept buzzing around me.

Feb. 17, Wednesday. Partly cloudy. Last night an owl was hooting and the cicadas chirping. The mosquitoes bothered me. I left early and reached the top of Pinacate Peak at 10 a.m., about an hour and a half from camp—a very easy climb from the north or west, all over smooth, easy slopes. A horse could be brought up from either direction. My barometer recorded 3,400 feet above Papago Tanks, the thermometer 73°F. in the shade. On top I found a monument, and in it a tin box with the cards of L. D. Ricketts and J. C. Greenway of Warren, Arizona, and that of R. J. Daniels, Bates Well, all March 23, 1914. I placed my own record in the cup.

I had looked carefully for sheep en route but saw none. I saw a robin on top, also hummingbirds, two red-tailed hawks, a raven, and the usual wrens. I caught and skinned a mouse on the peak. The Bigelow cholla grows on the north and south slopes to within 100 feet of the top, also two varieties of grass, stunted palo verde, greasewood, and a small flower and a few other weeds. I noticed several mouse holes. In an old pile of rocks I found 3 Indian arrowheads of obsidian. I saw three varieties of butterflies—white, yellow, and a multicolored one. Old sheep dung was scattered about. I had a vast sweep of the surrounding country, although a little hazy. With Lumholtz' map I could locate many features.

After lunch, I searched a vast stretch of country with my glasses and tramped about doing so, but did not see a sheep. This is discouraging, as I should have located some over such an extent of country. I tramped about the mountains all the p.m. but saw not a sheep or fresh sign. I did find an old ram's head near Pinacate Peak. It was well preserved and with aching shoulders I brought it to camp.

Just before reaching camp, on a ridge to the north, I saw a ewe and lamb feeding. It is going to be very difficult to find rams. I saw a roadrunner well up on the mountain near the peak. I love the mountains and the hunting, but I am, for the first time, homesick to see Louisa. I must keep at the hard work and maybe I will be rewarded.

Feb. 18, Thursday. Fine day, partly cloudy. I left early for the north end of the range. After going about a mile, I looked up and saw a ram of about seven years old on a ridge close to a high mountain, near where I saw the ewe and lamb last night. The ram was looking down at me. Soon I saw a lamb near it and knew that the ewe was also near. This is the same ram and same ewe and lamb that I disturbed on the top of the mountain Feb. 15th. I could do nothing but approach directly upward in full sight. When within 400 yards, the ram became nervous. I aimed and a misfire! He ran before I could try again. What is the matter with my rifle?

I climbed the big mountain and climbed up and down mountain after mountain on the north end of the range. At 2 p.m., on a little mountain 2 miles away, I saw five ewes feeding. I descended and started in that direction. Soon they lay down. I had a plain to cross, and then approached to within ½ mile in an arroyo, then I had to wait. After an hour they rose and quickly fled around the mountain out of sight. I started and had not gone far when I saw three more ewes on a low connecting ridge, going to the little mountain. I had to wait until they passed out of sight, and then again started. Then I saw three more ewes crossing along the same ridge. These are the ewes I disturbed Feb. 15th, joined by one or two others. When all had passed out of sight, I followed, climbed the little mountain, and found that all the ewes had crossed the lava field to some other mountain. I did not see them again. They were very wild and cautious and kept looking more than feeding. There was a yearling ram among them and he was the most suspicious and kept jumping on rocks and looking all the time. None of them saw or suspected me.

I had to start for camp and had an hour in the dark, tramping over the rough lava. This day has been still more discouraging. This is a big country and the sheep are scattered and very difficult to find, even when I can sweep vast areas with the glasses. Nearly every mountain is smooth on one or two sides, and even if the other sides are rough, all can be easily climbed. I have never hunted in a country where it is so easy to climb the mountains, but it is noisy on the loose lava. It has been a fine day and I have had wonderful vistas. This lava desert and the scenery grows on me. But when will I have success?

Feb. 19, Friday. Stormy. This morning raindrops began to fall before daylight, and I got up and started a fire and made more shelter. But the clouds blew over, and soon I started south in a heavy wind and under a threatening sky. It was cold and I could see little of the mountains all enveloped in mist. At 1 p.m. a very heavy storm came up as I was on a mountain. I crawled under an overhanging rock and made a fire of ocotillo and kept it going. The mist enveloped everything—for an hour I could not see 50 feet. The wind howled and raindrops fell.

After two hours the mist cleared and I tramped about the mountains but saw not a single sheep or fresh signs. I saw jack rabbits and I noticed their dung high up on the mountain. I reached camp at sunset and never have I seen such wonderful colors. I could look down on the desert, which was mantled-over with a wondrous red-lavender, surrounding it completely like a mist. The color was intense and behind it a golden sky. Then it changed to bright purple—the whole desert was illuminated. Then the colors faded, leaving a deep crimson sky.

I picked up an old ram's head—good skull, horns fine—down on the lava as I was returning to camp. One more day and then I must move south. Tomorrow I will take a hard tramp over the main range toward the north.

Saturday, Feb. 20. Very windy, partly cloudy. Just after daylight, before leaving this morning, I found a Costa hummingbird's nest half built in a small palo verde in front of camp. I was near the tree and saw the bird alight to construct it.

I went over the main range to the N.E. At the top of the first mountain I again saw the ewe and lamb and got within a hundred yards—I did not see the ram. I went over mountain after mountain all day on the east side of the range and did not see a sheep. I returned to camp at dark. In two places I found the bones of sheep. There has been little today except hard work. I must move farther south. I have never tramped over easier mountains and can cover long distances. Besides, I can hunt crestlines and sweep the field with glasses. It is clear that I am not where the sheep are feeding for the most part. But I am enjoying the days, and am thinking mostly of my family. Red-tailed hawks are common, also vultures, which I often see soaring in flocks high up. I have not seen a golden eagle.

Multi-headed barrel cactus. Charles Sheldon.

Sunday, Feb. 21. Clear, little wind. I spent three hours on the mountain north of camp but saw nothing. Win arrived about 10:30 and I mounted "Junk" and we rode S.W. on an old trail leading from up near Pinacate Mountain to the Tank de los Chivos, where Staley had moved our main camp. We arrived and I went over to the Chivos tank and found old Indian camps, very ancient. They had cleared the rocks off of more than an acre and there were many stones with hollows for pounding Indian wheat. We had passed another good tank two miles up the same canyon with a rock blind used by Indians for hunting sheep. Barrel cactus is very abundant in this region, growing all over the mountains. These mountains look very red, as does Pinacate Peak which is covered with red cinders. The giant cactus grows abundantly in the main range to within 3 or 4 hundred feet of the peak. It is not abundant outside of the lava, and is most abundant at elevations of 17 to 25 hundred feet above Papago Tanks.

Monday, Feb. 22. Perfect weather. After five and a half hours,

A clump of senita cacti growing in the lava. Charles Sheldon.

we reached the Tank of the Cuervo. We went on ³/₄ mile up to Galletal Tank, and came back and camped at Cuervo. We have passed around the south to the S.E. part of the range on an old Indian trail. After going 4 miles we found the fresh tracks of 5 or 6 burros and 2 unshod horses, then a small fire, still hot, indicating Mexicans were ahead—we did not catch them. Near the sand to the south we found many acres of thickly growing verbena, "pinking" the ground completely. It was very beautiful. We saw a couple of antelope tracks in the trail and a jack rabbit. The lava at the south end of the range is entirely different from that more to the north. It is in beds, smooth on the surface but much curled and wrinkled.

It has been a most fascinating ride in balmy weather, the ground covered with flowers, and the vast spaces surrounding us —the Pinacate on our left, distant desert mountains ahead, and wavy sand dunes on our right. We are little specks on this spacious surface of desert. I noticed gopher workings in the sand. According to Lumholtz, the trail Win and I followed over the mountain yesterday passes clear over to Emilia Tanks, south of the peaks.

Sounds of life on this desert of lava: at dawn the plaintive call of the Gambel partridge; then the songs of the rock wrens and mockingbirds; the songs of house finches and sage sparrows; the buzz and twitter of Costa hummingbirds; the chirp of phainopeplas; the swish and caws of ravens; and the harsh note of the western gnatcatcher. On the mountain the ravens are ever present, as are the hummingbirds, rock and canyon wrens, cactus wrens, and gnatcatchers.

Tuesday, Feb. 23. Fine day. I left at daybreak and tramped all day, up and down the south outside mountains, and did not see a sheep. Neither did I see a sheep trail on the mountains, only old beds and very little old dung. Compared with the signs on the west side, I should say sheep may stray out on these south mountains but do not regularly inhabit them. I could look out on the plain and see 100 or more wild burros. The organ pipe cactus invades the lava well up. The giant cactus is in its usual abundance and commonly grows, as it does all over the Pinacate, high up on the cliffs and rocks with apparently no soil. There has not been so much rain on the south side of the range. Win and Staley saw an antelope and two fawns not far from the camp. I am going over to Sierra Blanca for a night and experiment over there—the southernmost sierra of the Pinacates.

Wednesday, Feb. 24. Perfect weather. Win and I left early this a.m. and in 2 hours and 15 minutes reached Sierra Blanca, the most southern mountain of the Pinacate group. It is a granite range three or four miles long, saw-toothed and very rough—straight up and down with a sharp, ragged, knife-edge crestline. The display of primroses (white and yellow) and verbena and other flowers on a belt of sand which we crossed was wonderful. In some places the verbena covers square miles, and toward evening the ground is solid pink.

I soon climbed to the crest and went as far south along it as a husband with a wife and three children should, then descended and walked north around the mountain, reaching camp after dark. I saw some good signs of sheep, but not one animal. This mountain reminds me of the Gilas in every respect, except that it is a narrow range and has no long canyons. It is honeycombed and very dangerous and difficult to climb and clamber along. I had fine views all day. The *Elaphrium*, which is rare in the Pinacates, is abundant here.

Tonight the moon is almost full, it is absolutely calm, a coyote is yelling in the distance, and the cicadas are chirping. I am nestled-in at the edge of two mountains, with the vast desert in front of me. There are but few giant cactus here, but I notice a few large ones growing high, near and on the crests of the range. I am off before daylight tomorrow.

Thursday, Feb. 25. Fair, rain in the p.m. Last night two coyotes came up within 100 yards and kept yelling me awake. I left at daylight, tramped along the mountainside to the south end, 4 or 5 miles distant, and then climbed and "crested" the mountains north to a point where the crest was too broken. This makes the whole range crested but half a mile. I did not see a sheep, although a few are on the mountain. A well-defined trail goes along the crest and I find other trails and beds – the same as in the Gila range, but fewer. I saw no evidence of sheep feeding below, all high. I forgot my rucksack in my haste to get off, so I had this hard tramping until after five without food or water. About 2 p.m. I did see two doe antelope feeding along the base of a small mountain a little way out from the main range, but I would not shoot them. Along the bases of all these ranges, big and little, I notice antelope trails ten feet more or less up the slope. From the top of the south crest I could see the course of the Sonoita River going through the sand nearly to the Gulf. It undoubtedly enters there.

I got caught in the rain on my return and was soaked when I reached camp. I found Win there with the horses. I was very thirsty, but tea and some bread put me in trim and we rode back, reaching this camp at Cuervo Tank after dark. Just before arriving, we saw three large white-sided jack rabbits [antelope jackrabbits] and I tried to shoot one, but the rifle misfired, being wet and the spring too weak. The antelope that Win and Staley saw still remain here, feeding.

Watering the horses at Emilia Tanks. Charles Sheldon.

Friday, Feb. 26. Perfect weather. In six hours we reached the Tanks of Emilia. We took rather a more circuitous route than necessary. It has been a picturesque trip, riding up the lava directly toward Pinacate. We found a large tank and many old Indian camps 3 miles below here. We are camped 300 yards below the tanks, in the bed of an arroyo. No incident has marked the trip.

Saturday, Feb. 27. Extra-perfect weather. I left very early and went up the old Indian trail leading up to the east peak and over to Tank of the Chivos. John Greenway, Ricketts, and party had left a note in a can at Emilia Tank saying they took horses up this trail and passed the night on top, March 24, 1914. After an hour I came to the sacred cave of Iitoi [a Papago deity] and found that since Lumholtz was here [January 3, 1910] it has all caved in—nothing left but three pack rats' nests inside. The trail goes by the base of the cinder cone of the east peak within 1,000 feet of the top. I saw a robin and a cottontail rabbit. I shortly climbed the peak and built a monument. My barometer showed

Pinacate Peak as seen from the top of Carnegie Peak. Charles Sheldon.

3,100 feet, thermometer 62° in the shade. Ocotillos grow within 200 feet or less of the top on the south side. I could see no sheep. The climbing is a little difficult simply because the fine cinders give way. But from the west side it is very easy. Bigelow cholla grow densely within 100 feet of the top. I descended and climbed the intermediate peak, which I found, by signs, was a sheep pasture at some time, as is the whole country surrounding these peaks, the main group of mountains. I saw ten or eleven jack rabbits in the basin south of the peaks. A lake is formed here temporarily after a rain. The Bigelow cholla here grows more densely than I have seen it elsewhere, so dense that I had to dodge it constantly, especially the numerous pack rat nests [made of loose cholla joints] which are densely scattered every-

Crossing a lava field east of Pinacate Peak. Charles Sheldon.

where. I noticed two large sahuaros growing on the south slope of Pinacate within 100 or 150 feet of the top.

I went to the west edge of the lava and all day climbed up and down every mountain, overlapping my route on the other side, and not a sheep did I see. It is clear that practically all the sheep have left the main range of mountains. It has been a wonderful day, very clear. Thus I have tramped on every mountain of this group and the close outside mountains west and south. It looks discouraging. I must move again and there is only one place left. But the whole desert and mountains have taken hold of me.

Sunday, Feb. 28. Perfect weather. We left this morning with all the horses but with only enough material and water for my own camp. Win thought there was a trail through the lava to Elegante Crater and soon we got in a trough of lava and had a terrible time for three hours. It was very hard on the horses and Win's mare, "Pinkie," became very sick and she is in bad condition tonight. By degrees we worked through, but with the legs of the horses cut very badly. Shortly after, we stopped a mile from the Crater Elegante, on a sand flat washed by water, with greasewoods and a few sahuaros. After some tea, we started for the crater. On a small adjoining mountain we saw a ewe, then later a small ram. I circled and climbed, but they had run off.

Then I went to the crater. It is magnificent, almost a perfect circle, with an even rim except for some rising ground to the east. We soon located a ewe and lamb and a small ewe and a yearling ram feeding well up on benches between the upper cliffs. This crater contains a series of four perpendicular cliffs that circle clear around it, rising above short benches. The bottom has rising ground to the south. Staley and I started to find a way down from the south side. It was crag work and after finding a way to get down a cliff we circled the bench until we found a way to get down the next, etc. After laborious work we reached the talus slope, which, unlike the slope of the Sykes Crater, is filled with tremendous boulders.

We finally reached the bottom, which is not nearly so attractive as that of the Sykes Crater. It is a lake when it rains, and soon dries, so the bottom is sand, caked from water. At the lowest points there are still two pools of water four or five feet deep. Sahuaros, greasewoods (abundant), a few ironwood, mesquite, and palo verdes are there. No tree chollas, but a few organ pipe cactus scattered about. Vegetation is more scarce than in the Sykes. We paced it on the center diameter and I made 900 paces, Staley, independently, 911 paces.

It was late—dusk—and we started up the north side. We saw the yearling ram not far above and he offered good shots but soon ran out of sight. About halfway up, there was nothing but moonlight and a succession of cliffs ahead. We toiled upward and surmounted the cliffs until the last one. This was a problem. We had to go for several hundred yards along the bench until we finally found a place where, by dangerous crag work, we got up. Not far beyond was the main trail.

To descend this crater is crag work, but there are several places, perhaps many, where a person with courage can get down. My barometer shows the depth to be 685 feet. My moccasins had worn through and my stocking feet got full of cholla.

I had a hard time of it tramping back. Win and Staley left and I am here alone on the vast plain, with the brilliant sky above.

Monday, March 1. Heavy wind, showers in the p.m. Just after daylight I went to the crater and saw the three sheep feeding high up on a bench, also the old ewe with a lamb and the ram that were on the outside mountain. These latter had gone back in the crater. The ram was not over 4 years old. I went along the east rim of the crater, which is the highest. At this point the altitude from the bottom is 750 feet, and a fair average is 700 feet for the whole rim. The washed sand area is exactly in the center and the floor surrounding it is mostly fine cinders covered with greasewood, with sahuaros scattered sparingly. Some sahuaros grow on the cliffs. The upper slope extending down to the first cliff descends only about 50 feet, and here is how the Sykes Crater gets more depth—its corresponding slope is 150 feet. Yesterday I noticed a honey bees' nest on the highest cliff. Also we saw the tracks of the gray fox in the bottom. I saw a pair of hawks about the size of pigeon hawks flying about the crater and crying as if they had a nest in the cliffs. Altogether, the name Crater Elegante is most appropriate. It impresses one with its vastness and the perfection of the circle. But the bottom looks cold and inhospitable as compared with the Sykes. There are not as many Bigelow chollas as in the Sykes.

I went two miles N.E. and hunted a group of mountains, but found only very old sheep sign and nothing to indicate that sheep regularly inhabit them. Then I tramped 5 miles west, taking in a mountain en route, to another group in the lava, with the same result. Feed is scarce on all these outside mountains. It showered late and I went under some rocks but got wet just the same. The wind blew a gale all day.

I reached camp just after dark to find everything covered with sand—my camp is in a sand wash. I never felt more discouraged about finding rams. I will not shoot them in craters.

Tuesday, March 2. Cloudy, windy, and a few drops of rain. Cold. At 1:30 a.m. raindrops began to fall, the sky was black, and lightning flashed all around, followed by thunder. I jumped up, put my robe in the bag, covered everything up, and made a fire. The rest of the night I slept without shelter beside the fire. The rain kept threatening but did not fall.

After breakfast, I limped up on top of the peak south of the crater. I put on new moccasins yesterday and my toes are worn raw and I can scarcely walk. I photographed the crater. I could see no sheep in those parts I could look into. At noon I went to camp and the men soon arrived with the horses and the whole outfit and the bad news that during their absence the coyotes had eaten all the meat and the bacon and everything that had any grease in it. This puts us short of food. After eating a lunch of bread, we packed and started, and in 2½ hours arrived on the east-west divide of the main trend of the mountains, where I camped—they went on to Papago Tanks. Jack rabbits were extremely abundant on the plain.

Here I am in a picturesque spot, surrounded by walls of lava and fine mountains, with my camp in a wash among ironwood and palo verde trees. I have only two pails of water and little food. The moon has been full and the desert has been illuminated at night. Here it illumines the mountains, and the weird light surrounding me evokes more strongly my continual thoughts of loved ones. My feet now are a great handicap in tramping, but I must work, work, work, and find some sheep.

Wednesday, March 3. Perfect weather in the a.m., windy in the p.m. Last night there was a heavy frost and I found the water frozen in the pails. Yesterday we saw three piles of stones 2 miles below here, less than two hours from Crater Elegante, indicating a tank nearby in a lava canyon. A trail, much obliterated, leads to it from near the crater.

I started this morning for a mountain N.E. of this camp, and while climbing the slope I saw six sheep on a mountain 2 miles distant to the S.W., feeding near the crest. Although I could not make out their sex, I went for them at once. As I approached within a half a mile, I saw all six rapidly crossing a narrow flat, heading toward the lava leading to the main range—5 ewes and a small ram. I could not tell if lambs were with them. I climbed the mountain and circled the crest, but found no more sheep on it. Then, descending, I walked two miles north and climbed and crested a rather low, rough sierra for two hours, but there were no sheep on it. I saw much old sign on both mountains, and on the last, tracks, two or three days old, where two sheep had ascended and again where they left it for another mountain. It seems certain that at this time of year the sheep keep traveling, searching for a better food supply. There are many more signs on these northern mountains, indicating that at times sheep remain for some time on them.

My feet are so sore that I am really a cripple and have no business climbing the mountain crags, but I must keep on, hoping that luck will cause me to get a fair chance. This is really the last available territory and in another day I will cover it. The chances are slim. I am living on half rations, as the food supply is low.

Thursday, March 4. Beautiful day, windy in the p.m. Today my disappointment is complete, but the story is an interesting one. Soon after daylight, I started to climb the mountain in front of camp, which on the sides has fine cinder slopes covered with cholla, but on the inside of the circle is an old crater like most in this region, deep and the sides broken, with cliffs, boulders, and rugged slopes. Looking to the right, I saw a ram with what appeared to be an enormous head come down off the lava and cross to the mountain slope, too far for a shot. My glasses revealed big, massive horns, finer than I had ever expected to get. The ram went diagonally up the slope to the east and passed over the crest.

I immediately went around the mountain to the west and climbed up where the slope dips low and looked over into the broken center. Soon I saw the magnificent sight of the ram on a high rock at the N.E. summit of the crest, standing like a statue, looking. He kept looking for ten minutes and then stepped back out of sight. I waited for fifteen minutes, but he did not appear. Then I began the ascent along the crest and around the circle of the top. I put all the caution into it that I could, and finally reached the point where the ram had disappeared, without seeing anything. But looking down the slope, near the bottom, much too far for a shot, I saw the ram walking around the base of the mountain, not far up. It was not difficult to keep him in sight, since I had the advantage of the crest and the slope was practically unbroken. Gradually and aimlessly, the ram circled round until he came upon the crest at the lowest point, the exact place where I had first ascended. He looked the inside over for ten minutes, practically standing in my trail, then he stepped down ten feet to the edge of cliffs and lay down. This made a stalk a most difficult problem, for I could only approach around the steep, fine-cinder slope, which was slippery and noisy. But I had to attempt it.

I marked the spot by an ocotillo and sahuaro which were growing above on the crest, and started. I have never in my life used so much caution, knowing that the success of my whole trip depended on this stalk. Although punished by chollas, I gradually approached the spot. Then began the difficult part, step by step, arranging the ground for good footholds, watching should the ram suddenly appear. But I could not help making a little noise—the fine cinders would give in spite of everything I could do. But at last the critical moment came. I cocked the rifle, put it to my shoulder, and after getting a solid foothold gradually arose, immediately seeing the ram's magnificent horns. I stood up quickly. The ram had heard me and was standing broadside, looking at me, not 30 yards away. The bead of my rifle was on his shoulder. I quickly pulled the trigger and a *MISFIRE!*

As I threw the bolt for another try, the ram jumped over the cliff. When I reached the spot, he was not in sight, having passed immediately over into a canyon. But soon he emerged, high up across the other side, too far for a shot. Soon his horns passed over the skyline. He was gone and I was defeated. But it was an earned chance and I am just as proud of the stalk as if I had killed him. I feel a certain satisfaction in having run down a big ram after days of tramping and hard work.

Was I careless to have come without being sure as to the working of the rifle? I sent the rifle to Abercrombie and Fitch (agent for Jeffery rifles) to put on new sights, thoroughly repair it, and put everything in perfect order, with special instructions to be sure as to the lock. Also, I had them send the rifle to the

Stoeger Company to test the sights, and the cartridges were sent for that purpose. The report was, "O.K."

The first shot attempted here, the rifle went off. The next two were misfires. I took the lock apart and found everything apparently all right. I have noticed that in this climate the lock was a little sticky in the morning. Regularly each morning before going out I have taken out the lock and dried it and cleaned off all dust or sand. I could have done no more. I tested it at the Chivos Tanks camp and it went off for five shots with solid bullets made in the U.S. But now I only have new German soft-nose cartridges with brass primers and these may require more force than the old cartridges available at the time the rifle was made. The spring may be a little weak. More likely the firing pin is worn. Really, I take more satisfaction in having made two deliberate, well-earned stalks at good rams, losing them to the misfires, than I would have taken had I killed two rams by luck and chance without the earned stalks.

I went on and climbed a big mountain to the N.W. Sheep sign was abundant, mostly old. Yet, some sheep had been there recently—I saw none. It is clear that most of the sheep of this region are to the north, northwest, and a few west of the main group of mountains. They are very restless, traveling from mountain to mountain. I reached camp just before dark, as dark clouds covered the sky above the mountain north of camp, while a brilliant rainbow encircled the mountain. A mockingbird hopped about camp, picking up bits, and almost allowed me to catch it.

Friday, March 5. Perfect weather. Early this morning I limped up the mountain where the ram was lost, but I saw nothing. For the last two days I have seen cranes flying north. About 1 p.m. Win arrived and we took an old but well-marked Indian trail leading from the tank previously mentioned to the Papago Tanks. This trail joins the main trail from Agua Dulce about two miles above the Papago Tanks, where we arrived in 2½ hours.

Then I took my rifle lock apart and studied the whole mechanism. I find that at the first snap of the trigger the cap does not explode, but after throwing out the cartridge, the succeeding ones go off. It seems that the ejection apparatus is defective, but I cannot say why. But there is lost motion so that at the first snap the firing pin does not go home.

Yesterday Win and Staley went to a small granite mountain at the edge of the sand and killed two mature ewes, so we have plenty of meat. In one old ewe Win found an embryo not over a month old. As in Alaska, here some of the sheep breed irregularly

Saturday, March 6. Perfect weather. Pinkie, Win's mare which I rode last year, had a fall at the Emilia Tanks the day I left and has been sick and not eaten since. The horses were put out to feed a mile away. This morning at 4, in the moonlight, Pinkie staggered into camp, breathing heavily. She came close to us, tottered and fell over. After a few moments, she rose, went a short distance, and fell over and died. It was pathetic.

I left early and went to the Sykes Crater. It is higher on the south rim, and on the whole about the same depth as the Elegante. But being so much smaller, when one looks straight down, the depth is more impressive. Then I hunted the Rainbow Ridge carefully and saw no fresh sign and not much old until at the east end of it. I hunted the mountains beyond until I joined the line where I had already hunted, but saw nothing but old sign, although two or three sheep had wandered over there within two weeks. But on a small mountain 2 miles to the east, at 5 p.m., I saw a single ewe feeding near the crest.

At six, Staley came along the trail with the horses and we rode six miles, reaching camp at dark. The interesting thing is that in a wash 4 miles east of here we saw the tracks of a big mountain lion, only three or four days old. So lions inhabit this country, or at least stray into it. We took two cottontail rabbits in traps today. I have only one more chance and that is at Hornaday Mountain, and this is very doubtful, but if my feet will permit, I must try it. They are very sore tonight. I have steeped them in tea made of the leaves of the greasewood. The men have gone off to sleep near the horses, and I am here alone.

Sunday, March 7. Perfect weather. This morning I found that my feet were in such condition that it was out of the question to attempt to climb mountains today, so the morning was spent about camp. There is a honey bees' hive in the rocks above the tank, but the honey cannot be obtained without dynamite. Coyotes sprang all the traps last night without getting in one. A quail got caught in one and a coyote came along and ate it. No vultures have yet observed the dead horse, but the ravens and coyotes are preparing for us to leave camp.

In the afternoon Win came and I moved to within a mile of Hornaday Mountain. He went back so I am again alone. I observed the Molina and MacDougal craters en route. I am camped alongside the MacDougal, which is a fine, large crater, although not very deep. The desert is beautiful with flowers — I have collected many. Tomorrow I shall make my last try to find a ram on the mountain. My wife and the little ones at home are ever present in my thoughts.

Monday, March 8. Perfect weather. I rose at 5 a.m. and left in the darkness for the extreme east end of Hornaday Mountain, determined to walk the whole three miles of crestline and hunt the spurs as thoroughly as I could. Hornaday Mountain is at the edge of the sand and is thoroughly honeycombed like the Gilas, but the crestline is comparatively easy to clamber along, although there are many pinnacles which are very dangerous and some have to be rounded. At other places the crest makes a knife-edge. Yet the whole can be covered by one with experience among the crags.

I reached the east end at MacDougal Pass before daylight and had to wait until it was light enough to start. At last the dawn came, with the singing of the wrens and croaks of the ravens and the call of the quail — a beautiful rosy dawn. The primroses, both yellow and white, and all the other luxuriant flowers of the sand took on their color and I started upward along a low ridge. I soon reached the high mountain and by degrees I went up into the crags and at last was high on the crest. Then the hunt was fairly on.

I went out on the spurs and took every opportunity to see as

MacDougal Crater as seen from the crest of the Hornaday Mountains. Charles Sheldon.

many spots on the honeycombed slopes as possible. Up and down I climbed, ascending to the crest and descending, many times having to sling my rifle. At about nine-thirty, as I walked out on a spur, I suddenly saw two ewes and one lamb well up near the crest, within easy shot. I watched them but did not shoot. The lamb of the other ewe soon joined her. They were extremely cautious and watched as much as any sheep I have ever seen. They disappeared in a little canyon on the side-slope and I went on.

I do not think that any other mountain here is situated so that the panorama is so beautiful from the crest. On the north is the sand, shining with flowers, the vast belt of sand stretching around to the west. A line of rugged mountains swings east from the north end of this mountain, with short gaps, to the Tuserals, which rise mysteriously across the sand. The Pinta range is still farther to the east and other ranges fade away in that direction. Toward the N.W. is the Sierra Nina, and beyond the Sierra de Viejo and Sierra de Lechuguilla. And far to the west, in the sand, is El Rosario, standing dimly all alone. To the south is the desert bordering Hornaday Mountain, full of sahuaros and ocotillos, the washes lined with palo verdes and ironwoods. A half mile beyond lies MacDougal Crater, appearing like a vast hole in the earth. Still farther beyond is the lava and the Pinacates. Sand hill cranes were continually flying over all day toward the Gulf.

With such a panorama before me, I kept on, hour after hour. Sometimes the crest dips low, which means a difficult descent and a long ascent. I stopped for lunch on a little peak, and then, after a cigarette, continued on. About two p.m. I saw another ewe within shot below me, and I suspected her lamb was near, lying down. She at last looked up and saw me and at once ran down in a canyon and disappeared. I shortly after reached the highest crestline of the mountain and went out on many spurs but I saw no rams.

At four-thirty I reached the highest peak of the mountain, 1,175 feet above camp by my barometer, and then sat down to inspect the slopes. Soon, just below the crest, very near the west end of the mountain, I saw three rams — two good ones and one smaller. They were nearly $3/4$ of a mile away. I studied the crestline, and planned to stalk them by going out on a spur near where they were quietly feeding. I slipped out of sight and started and "crested" as rapidly as possible, perhaps taking too many chances, but I knew the success of my trip depended upon this chance. I looked at my rifle, tried to tighten the extractor, and felt that it would go off.

After nearly an hour I was near the spur, and at last went out on it and found the slope very rough. But the rocks made little noise and finally, at just five-thirty, I was to the last 100 feet and went step by step, climbing upward on the slope. I came to some loose rocks and had to arrange them with my hands. Finally I crawled a few feet upward on my stomach, paused to take breath, took a glance out at the sand belt and scenery beyond, and gradually elevated my head and saw the three rams, not seventy-five yards away, feeding in full sight without any suspicion.

Selecting the one I thought had the largest horns, I carefully aimed and pulled the trigger and a misfire. I was prepared and quickly threw in another cartridge as quietly as possible. But one of the rams heard the bolt of the rifle, for it jumped up and looked toward me. But I had the bead on his shoulder and the report answered the pull of the trigger. The ram dropped and lay almost suspended in air, as they were feeding on an almost perpendicular, cliffy slope. The other two rushed upward a little way, and as they stopped a moment I fired at the largest and he dropped and fell downward along the side of the broken cliff. I tried to cover the third ram with the bead as he ran along the side of a slope, and at last fired and he staggered with a broken hind leg and climbed for some distance, and then fell – the bullet had entered his vitals from behind.

I had little time. I went to the first ram and photographed him, then the second, and then the third. It took me fifteen minutes to find the second one, as he had fallen down fifty feet and wedged between two rocks on a practically perpendicular slope, but broken so I could get up and down. Then I went to work and skinned the first ram. At least 30 vultures appeared, circling above, and two ravens alighted on the third ram. At 6:30 I had the skin off and, putting it and the head in my rucksack, went to the second, hastily took out his insides, and put my red handkerchief over his head. I went to the third and after dressing him, piled rocks about his head so the vultures would not damage it.

I was on the north slope of the crest and before I had climbed to the summit it was dark. Then there was a steep, dangerous canyon to go down. I cut a staff from a bayonet plant [agave] and then, with a heavy load on my back, began that most dangerous of all mountain tasks – descending in the dark. Step by step, with uncertainty and danger at every moment, constantly wounded by Bigelow chollas, I kept on, and what would have required half an hour in daylight took me over two hours. Then came the relief of danger passed, and the long tramp of three miles across the cactus desert.

I reached my camp at 11:30 p.m., cooked some liver of one of the rams, and now write these notes. Thus success crowns all my long, hard, discouraging work for over a month. But I have at last killed rams by an earned stalk, high up on the crest of a rugged mountain. Now back to my dear wife and children as fast as possible.

Evening primroses near the Hornaday Mountains. Charles Sheldon.

Tuesday, March 9. Perfect weather. At daylight I was off, after leaving a note for Win to meet me with the pack horses at the west end of the mountain. I climbed over the crest and found that the vultures had not touched the sheep, but that coyotes had eaten practically the whole hindquarters of the second one killed. I took his head and scalp and then the skin and head of the third. The sheep were on such steep, broken ground that the work was slow. But by noon I met the men at the bottom of the mountain, and after a cup of tea we packed, crossed the sand, and here we are at my lone camp of a year ago, surrounded by the rugged Tuseral Mountains.

The display of flowers on all sides of Hornaday Mountain is more wonderful than can be described, as it is throughout the sand belt. It is a garden of white primroses banked thick everywhere. And clustered densely around trees and cactus are verbena and tall red flowers and smaller white and yellow flowers and ajo lillies, making this vast garden which must be one of the most impressive displays of flowers this country provides. I rode through it feeling as if in a fairyland. It is an impressive sight, coming up here from the sand with the Sierra Nina and the Tuserals on both sides. I was familiar with the crests and peaks, and many a tramp they recalled.

There are mosquitoes here—I have not been bothered with them since leaving Crater Elegante. The tracks of four more rams were seen at the extreme west end of Hornaday Mountain. Not a sheep track about here in these arroyos—all the sheep are high in the mountains.

Wednesday, March 10. Showers in the a.m., overcast. This morning at five we were all aroused by rain and sat by the fire in the dark during the showers. The horses were taken to Sheldon Tank for water, then we had breakfast. We came without incident to Tule Tank. At the tank Win picked up a very large, old, weather-beaten ram's head, which I am sending to Washington. It has been a cloudy, raw day. The desert up here is a little greener and has more flowers than when I came down, but we have passed the luxurious flowers. One day nearer my dear Louisa.

Thursday, March 11. Perfect weather. We reached Copper Mountain at six p.m., a fine ride during a perfect, cool day. While stopping for lunch I found a Costa hummingbird's nest in a small palo verde, with two young about a week old. The bird showed some alarm but soon flew away. I notice that the sahuaros do not often invade up the slopes through these granite ranges—cases of it are rare. It is quite the opposite in the Pinacates, where most of them are high on the mountains. The desert is mostly green. The greasewood about here is blooming with its pretty yellow flower, *Encelia* is all in bloom, and there are many other flowers, but not nearly so many as south of the Tule Tanks and alongside of the Cabeza Prieta range. Tomorrow I head for Wellton and the trip is ended.

Friday, March 12. Perfect weather. This morning I started at eight and galloped most of the way into Wellton, reaching there in $2\frac{1}{2}$ hours to find word that all is well at home.

Aerial view of the Sierra del Rosario in a sea of sand. Peter L. Kresan.

4

EXPEDITION TO THE SIERRA DEL ROSARIO, SONORA, 1916

The Sierra del Rosario is a series of jagged granitic peaks about 10 miles southwest of the southern end of the Tinajas Altas Mountians and 40 miles east of the Colorado River. Surrounded by a belt of sand dunes, the Sierra del Rosario rises nearly perpendicular to the desert floor, with the highest summit reaching an elevation of 1,820 feet. Isolated and without permanent water, the Sierra del Rosario is the most arid mountain range in North America.

In the spring of 1910, ethnologist Carl Lumholtz, accompanied by two Papagos named Pancho and Pedro, made a visit to the Sierra del Rosario — reportedly the first non-native to do so. While conducting his survey of the sierra, Lumholtz noted fresh tracks of mountain sheep and reported his observation in a book on his travels, New Trails in Mexico, published in 1912. Charles Sheldon, who had seen the mountain while hunting in the Tinajas Altas and Hornaday mountains, was intrigued. Might not the sheep in such an isolated and waterless range be a form new to science? Encouraged by his friends in the U.S. Biological Survey, Sheldon set out for the Sierra del Rosario in the spring of 1916 to collect specimens. Win Proebstel and Staley Hovatter were again hired to provide transportation between the railroad station at Wellton, Arizona, and the hunting grounds.

Sheldon managed to kill one sheep after a difficult hunt. From measurements of Sheldon's dwarfish adult bighorn ram and the skull of a ewe Sheldon picked up, C. Hart Merriam described the small sheep population in the Sierra del Rosario (fewer than ten animals by Sheldon's estimate) as belonging to a new species, Ovis sheldoni. Subsequent taxonomists, noting environmentally induced dwarfism in other individual sheep specimens and that the ewe's skull is within the range of measurements taken from other desert bighorn sheep, reclassified Ovis sheldoni as Ovis canadensis mexicana, the same race of desert sheep found in the neighboring mountain ranges of Sonora and southwest Arizona. Biologists also now know that male desert bighorn will travel many miles across broad valleys, thus precluding genetic isolation

A red-tailed hawk's nest in a lone saguaro cactus south of Wellton, Arizona. Charles Sheldon.

in even remote mountain ranges. Nonetheless, it is interesting that a sheep population existed in these arid and barren mountains 18 miles from the nearest permanent water. Even cacti are rare in the Sierra del Rosario, and where these sheep obtained their moisture is difficult to say.

March 3, 1916. The sky was dull and leaden, no air was in motion, and the desert was parched as the sun poured its heat through the hazy air and beat upon us as we traveled over the road to Tinajas Altas. There has been scarcely any rain this winter, and all the smaller tanks are said to be dry. It has been unusually hot. We left Wellton at noon, Win, Staley, three mules, and "Old Bill" (same as last year). I rode "Dink." Abundant lizards skittered about, horned toads were very common, birds were not very much in evidence. Late in the p.m. we passed between some hills and saw a red-tailed hawk's nest 15 feet up in a sahuaro. By driving up the wagon and building up the boxes, Win reached it and took two eggs. The hawk was sitting on the nest and we approached to 75 feet before she went off, flew high, soaring at a distance. She did not approach as we took the eggs. She was a dark slate-colored phase. Soon Old Bill became sick, unable to pass water. I saw one small yellow butterfly. The various points of the Gilas were familiar and I recalled my difficult climbing for sheep two years ago. We passed one flock of 7 Gambel's partridges, but no hummingbirds were observed. Win tells me that he was at the Sierra Pinta and tracks were numerous but sheep scarce. At eleven p.m. we camped a mile north of the tinajas.

March 4. There was a man camping at Tinajas Altas last night who left early this a.m. The morning was spent getting water— filling a 50-gallon can, two old oil cans, and three water bags— and caching most of the stuff. In the p.m. Win and I started. I rode ahead to Surveyor Tank, which was entirely dry. Then we turned a little north, and then west, and came to the extreme northwest point of Republic Mountain—a high, irregular mountain mass extending west of the Gilas from Surveyor Tank. The whole desert is parched—nothing green except the usual desert shrubs which are always in their various shades of green. Many migrating flocks of small birds were seen, singing all the time. Hummingbirds were plentiful. Some *Encelia* is in bloom, a few flowers here and there. A crimson-flowered shrub [chuparosa], very abundant along the washes, is in full bloom and very lovely. There are practically no other flowers. The galleta grass is all dead, but now and then a little patch is found with a few green blades. I saw a number of jack rabbits. As I approached

Win Proebstel en route to the Sierra del Rosario. Charles Sheldon.

the end of the point of Republic Mountain, Sierra del Rosario loomed up out on the desert, a rugged, jagged crestline of rough mountains, appearing from a distance like a section of the Gilas. It was very hot. The night was so warm that we did not sit by the fire. My hands and neck are badly sunburned.

March 5. Rather cloudy and cool in the a.m., hot in the p.m. We started at nine and pulled up at the base of Rosario Mountain at 12:45, about 10 miles from the nearest point of Republic Mountain. We went very fast for two hours. We carried food, two 5-gallon cans of water, and two 5-gallon water bags. Soon we reached sand with scattered desert vegetation. A yellow flower was everywhere. In one or two spots *Pachylophus* [evening primrose] was blooming, but not brilliantly. The greasewood was in bloom, many of them. The sand became softer, the vegetation more scattered, and we were impeded by rat and gopher holes. Then two or three miles of clear, soft sand dunes, then sand with vegetation until we reached the wide wash near the mountain. Then 1/2 mile more and we made camp in a wash

The central section of the Sierra del Rosario. The trees in the foreground are ironwoods. Charles Sheldon.

right against the point of the mountain. I saw a nighthawk or whippoorwill. In a hollow between the dunes I found small fragments of fossil bones scattered over sixty or seventy feet of area, and collected some of them. A fox track was seen on the dunes.

After taking a cup of tea, Win left and I went north and around a big basin in the mountain and climbed up in several places. I saw very old sheep dung and old tracks here and there, but nothing else. Cactus was nearly absent—I saw only one Bigelow cholla and one other small *Opuntia* [cholla]. So far, this mountain is exactly like the Gilas. There is much yucca on the slopes, also *Elaphrium*. Ironwood trees are abundant near the washes, but only a few palo verde trees, except low along the washes. I only saw one fox track, and there are very few birds about. At least I know now that sheep have been here, but it is going to be very difficult to get them.

I reached camp at dark, a wonderful sunset covering the whole sky east and west. Tomorrow I start the hard hunting. The wind roars tonight.

March 6. Today I went around the south end of the main mountain, through the pass between this and the extreme south range, and around about midway, then climbed over to the other side and returned to camp in the dark. All day since daylight, with the exception of half an hour for lunch, I have tramped and hunted in a scorching sun. Twice I climbed to the crest, my barometer reading 1,550 feet above camp. I passed along the crestline for short distances, but it is impossible to go far. These mountains are more ragged on the crestline than the Gilas. A few very old, small sheep tracks here and there along the base, and dung (two months old) and old beds high up are all I have seen. A few small sheep have been about. No cactus of any kind except two very small *Opuntias*. Galleta grass and *Encelia* grow high up. There is some *Ephedra* [Mormon tea], and *Elaphrium* is very abundant. A few fairly large palo verde trees are along the big wash at the south end. Ironwood is everywhere—no signs of sheep feeding on it or anywhere below.

I was in perilous positions climbing about and had to cut a yucca staff and sling my rifle. I have no right to attempt such work with a family which I love so dearly and always keep thinking about. I saw a flicker, two nighthawks, a raven, two or three kinds of flycatchers, hummingbirds, three vultures, two kinds of hawks, and a few other small birds. Bird life is scarce. Lizards, even small ones, are seldom seen, and lizard dung is scarcely seen above. A few cottontail rabbits are in the washes. One coyote track, now and then an antelope squirrel, mouse sign in the washes, a scarce pack rat nest in the rocks, that is about all I have seen. I could not see the Gulf from above. It is very hot and another gale of wind tonight. It is doubtful that I can find these few sheep.

March 7. This morning, as I was eating breakfast just at daylight, a coyote came trotting across the wash just above camp. He stopped opposite me, fifty feet away, and watched broadside as I took out the rifle, aimed, fired, and to my astonishment, missed. He ran a short distance and stood until a third shot, when he ran. I fired again. All four shots missed, to my disgust. I looked at the sight and found it up at 300 yards! I will have this Rigby sight changed as it is too uncertain.

I left and went directly to the far south end of the mountain,

A Bigelow nolina in bloom. Charles Sheldon.

about two or three miles, past where the south section is separated from the main range by a half mile of flat. At the extreme south end, at the foot of a slope, I found the skull of a ewe, fairly well preserved. Passing around to the other side, my eye caught a familiar sight on the skyline of a peak—a sheep just passing over. My glasses revealed a two-year-old ewe. She jumped down from a rock and came running down what appeared to be a perpendicular slope and quickly passed out of sight, although once she paused to browse. I was surprised to see her indifference to the perilous slope.

I was soon climbing again, around the crest of a connecting spur, risking my life and I have no right to do it. Yet, I am more cautious than I once was. At last I was at the right point but could see nothing—all the surface is honeycombed. I climbed the peak and continued all day about the crest of the south end, but did not see the ewe again, nor any other sheep. The signs seemed to show that not more than one or two sheep have occupied this south range. Yet it was a wonderful day, with views of the beautiful high peaks of Rosario, the sand dunes, the distant vague stretch of desert on the west, the haze over the Gulf, and the mountains across it just visible. Pinacate—dark blue—was clearly visible in whole outline to the east, as were the Viejos and Gilas (their whole length) and other ranges in the north. A rather strong wind blew. Vultures hovered about. Two red-tailed hawks and two other hawks, swallows, and a flycatcher were seen. The rock and canyon wrens, though here, are not as common as elsewhere. I saw a raven catch a lizard in the rocks along the crest.

I was glad to be safe at the foot of the mountain at sunset—a glorious sky, the purple and pink glow covering the whole heavens. I tramped back to camp in the dark. Now I am sure that sheep are here. At the foot of the main range, well around toward this end, I saw the fresh tracks of a ewe and lamb crossing to the north mountain. It is quite possible that the ewe I saw picked up her lamb and came down one of the numerous canyons of the mountain and crossed over. The sheep are very scarce.

March 8. Extremely hot in the sun. Early I went to the south mountain and soon saw sheep tracks, small tracks of a ram or two. The sand butts up against the south end. After circling clear around, I saw a ram on the crest of the main range, watching me. He seemed small. I chose a spur and began the ascent. After a while the crest of the spur became more dangerous, but I kept on and when near the main crest, the cliffs fell downward and I could not proceed. Nor could I descend the slope. I had to retrace my steps and lost three hours, but I was satisfied to get down alive.

I could see no other ascent, so I continued around the mountain. I came back by the west side, climbing all the canyons and watching, but did not see another sheep and only a few signs. The two or three rams here seem to be where I have been today, but how to get them when I cannot go above, I don't know. There is practically no cactus on Rosario. I have only seen a few, five or six stunted *Opuntias*. Two jack rabbits were seen today, and the usual hawks and birds. It has been scorching hot. I reached camp after dark – tired.

March 9. This morning I was up at four, cooked breakfast, tramped two miles to the section of the mountain where I saw the ram, and waited half an hour for the daylight. I watched for a while and then found a route and, at the risk of life, climbed to the crest. As I looked over I saw three vultures lying on their stomachs on the side of a cliff with their wings spread out. They seemed to be asleep. Though a hundred yards below me, I tried a photograph. I could only proceed a hundred yards along the crest when cliffs stopped further progress. Behind, where I had started, were cliffs. I saw nothing, and descended over a perilous route down the other side, cliff work nearly all the way. I have never seen or been in mountains so broken and rough as these.

Reaching camp at noon, I found Win there with more water. After a cup of tea, he left and I went north and spent the afternoon among the mountains, but saw nothing. The sun is terribly hot. Flies buzz by the millions. I saw two cottontails and a large black bumble bee. I am to stay four more days. My chance of getting that ram is small – it will only be by luck, like finding a needle in a haystack, but I shall keep working.

March 10. No wind, intolerably hot at midday. At five-thirty I started across the desert for the north end of the main mountain to look for the ram. I could scarcely see the ground. The desert air was delightfully cool. The buzz of the hummingbirds sounded among the shrubs with the red flowers along the washes. Now and then the prolonged whistling chirp of insects made music, and the peeping of birds indicated the awakening of life. Several nighthawks flashed from under ironwood trees, and the cry of the small hawk, so common among the mountains, rang out against the silence. The long Gila and Viejo ranges soon became clearly outlined in the distance, and Pinacate, black in relief over the sand dunes, was more clearly visible than in the dancing waves of heat later in the day. Soon a great crimson semicircle over the lower end of the Viejos indicated the rising sun. Later it was tinged with gold, then the peaks of Rosario first caught the light and glowed in purplish hue. Then a great crimson ball began to appear, surrounded by a circle of pink and gold, and soon the whole globe of the sun rose above the rugged Viejo crest. Purplish hues overspread the desert, the sand dunes were golden, and a vague, indefinable tint of color filled the atmosphere. For fifteen minutes or more, while this silhouette of the rising sun was visible, the exquisite glow of color, the cool air, the calm, the pervading mystery of the wild desert, all were a tribute to this sun and it did not seem possible that a little later, like a fierce tyrant, it would send down its scorching rays and lash me with intolerable heat, and that my whole will power would be put to the test to endure it.

By the time the shining light rays had appeared and illumined the mountains, the air began to hum with the myriads of flies that now are so incredibly abundant as to cause continuous annoyance. I climbed the mountain at a point half a mile south of where I had seen the ram. I found a means of ascent up through the furrowed slope, but the steep water course, like all others here, made the ascent real crag work. As I neared the top, the last two hundred feet became perilous, but with the rifle slung on my back I kept on upward, wondering how I would find a way to proceed. These mountains are so broken that, when one is hunting, every ten feet brings new areas into view and one must pause and watch. I have accustomed myself to climb as noiselessly as possible, always selecting each rock or surface to place each footstep. Therefore, progress was very slow, yet when I reached the crest I was weltering in perspiration. No breeze greeted me with its delicious cooling effect.

In the saddle the surface was smooth and there were tracks of a ram, and dung—very fresh—indicating that he had passed this morning, shortly before my arrival. Both tracks and dung were small, of the same size that I had seen elsewhere on the mountain, and I was certain that they were made by the same ram I had seen. The displaced rocks and freshly thrown dirt up along the narrow crest to the south indicated his course. I could look down on both sides, almost perpendicular, and could view only very limited areas of the chaotic, rocky, furrowed slopes. My eagerness and strained watching were intense as I followed, but the crestline soon became pure crag work, and I had to slowly work along cliff walls, step by step. Here and there I could straddle the crest and look down sheer cliffs for several hundred feet on both sides. A vulture was soaring along the crest, two red-tailed hawks were also soaring about, and the small crying hawk was flying about the side of the mountain. Two ravens now and then swished by overhead and my presence did not seem to excite any of their usual curiosity, nor did it that of the vulture or hawks. These birds probably have never before seen a man up among these mountaintops. In such moments as these, one watches these birds with the deepest envy, realizing how easily they float about and see the ram that I, in continual danger, am looking for at less than a snail's pace.

The crest became even more difficult, and I had almost decided to stop and not attempt to go farther, but a displaced stone indicated the ram had gone ahead and I followed. At last I was on a little pinnacle, not a foot wide, above an abrupt cliff 20 feet high which terminated in a little saddle with a smooth surface—an old, unused sheep bed. There I could see the tracks of the ram where he had jumped from the side of the cliff, and just beyond the displaced rocks and fresh dirt where he had started up the wall of the peak ahead, the highest peak of this section of the mountain. Before I saw the tracks, I had decided the ascent of this peak was impossible. The narrow crest rose up a hundred and fifty feet, almost vertical, with sheer slopes falling away on each side. But when I saw the tracks of the ram going up, I studied it and, provided the rock was not too loose, felt there was a possibility of ascending it.

I went back and found a way (hazardous) around and down to the saddle, and once there the ascent to the peak looked impossible. Yet, I pondered long. Perhaps, if I should start, a possible way might be found. I could at least go up ten feet. The success of my whole trip probably depended on my getting to that peak. Slinging my rifle, I went up the ten feet. The rock was fairly firm. I found that I could go another ten feet. I did so, and went still farther. Each advance caused me to try to go up still farther. Then I could not turn around and had to keep on, almost straight up along a knife edge. I was clinging to a wall of rock with steep, perpendicular slopes falling away on either side. The whole aspect of the mountain was so savage that it required all my courage not to become nervous and make a false step or take hold of a loose rock. While I was clinging to the rock with both hands, not even daring to look down, a vulture soared easily and gracefully overhead, right up along the crest. I had the feeling that if I ever reached the top safely, it would be my last perilous attempt in these mountains, realizing strongly the claims of my dear wife and family. I worked upward, twice feeling that all had ended, yet I reached the top and then lay flat on my back in the broiling sun and closed my eyes to get relief from the strain I had undergone.

At last, cooled down and courage regained, I sat up and looked around. The top of the peak was fairly broad and I could easily walk about. All sense of danger soon passed. Three spurs fell away from the peak to the east. On only one could an attempt be made to go along its crestline. I saw a possible means of descent down a furrowed watercourse. There was no sign of the ram's tracks—where had he gone? His descent on this side of the peak was almost impossible—the slopes on all sides were precipices. My only chance, and this was undertaken with great disappointment, was to sit, endure the sun, and watch. Even then I felt, should the ram be seen, he would probably be in a place where I could not stalk him, or if he was killed, he would fall where I could not find him or get to him. But I sat there and moved about so as to bring all possible areas in view for two and a half hours and not a sign of him did I see. It was 12 noon. I was feeling the sun, so I started toward the canyon in order to descend a little way, find a rock where I could get in the shadow, and wait for two or three hours while the ram would probably be lying down. Then I would ascend and resume the watch.

As I started toward the point of descent, my eye caught something in motion about four hundred yards out on a spur, just below the crest, and I saw the ram pass over a rock and disappear. In less than three seconds he appeared on the only spur with a ragged crestline along which I could proceed. The ram was on the north slope. As I started to "crest" the spur, I knew that the whole success of my trip depended on my resolution to do my utmost in careful and noiseless walking and alert watching. I had carefully marked the spot. No opportunity to watch the points near it was missed. Many difficulties and some dangers were experienced as I advanced. Even with my eagerness and excitement, I was punished by the sun.

I came to within one hundred and fifty yards without having caught sight of the ram. Then I selected a good point and waited, watching for a few moments. He did not appear. About fifty yards ahead was a little pinnacle on the crest that offered a good chance to inspect ahead. I made for it with extreme caution and practically no noise, the rock being firm. This was the first time among these mountains when I did not have to pause every few steps and inspect all new areas. I watched only ahead, the possible point where the ram might appear. As I reached the pinnacle, conical and sharp pointed, I paused to get breath and then had to sling my rifle to ascend it. Reaching the top, I could see nothing in the way of a ram at the expected spot. The slope fell away very sheer in precipices among broken surfaces, boulders, and ravines. On both sides of me were the jumbled masses of rocks lifting up into the form of mountains. The wavy sand dunes stretched in a circle around the mountain, then beyond, the flat parched desert and the long line of the Viejos, while Hornaday Mountain and the blue Pinacate appeared blurred in the distance through the heat waves. A small hawk flew overhead and soared across to the next spur, all the time uttering its cries.

Then after a few moments the ram suddenly jumped up in sight on a rock ten feet beyond where I had seen him before and

Sheldon climbed this peak to collect a ram. Charles Sheldon.

stood rigidly, looking downward. He seemed very small but his horns had a fine curl. He blended somewhat with the gray rocks beyond him. I shot and heard the bullet strike him. He reared and then brought his forefeet down hard on the rock. My cartridges all fell out as I tried to pump in a new one, each sticking, owing to badly made clips. I pushed one in by hand. He still stood on the rock and at the next shot he humped up in such a way that I knew I had hit his belly. Quickly pushing in another cartridge by hand, I fired and he fell, having received a bullet squarely in the heart. He rolled downward and disappeared.

I hurried forward, fearing that he might have rolled into some inaccessible place. Arriving, I saw that, although in a very steep furrow of broken rock, he had been caught and held by a yucca a hundred yards below, where he lay dead. I simply sat down, lighted a cigarette, and enjoyed that supreme exultation always following the successful stalk of a ram, with the additional satisfaction of feeling that now my trip was a success. Then I worked downward to him. The first shot had struck him three inches below the spine but above the heart. Already the air was one hum with the flies around him. The slope was very steep, the rock very loose. After photographing him as best I could as he lay, I went down and selected the best spot I could find and dragged him down, 50 yards below, nearly losing him as the rocks began to slide. Then I ate a piece of bread and drank almost a canteen-full of water. The sun blazed hotter and hotter. The air became stifling. I measured him as best I could on such difficult ground. He seemed to be very small—a ram four years old with compact, curling horns proportionately massive. I suspect that owing to isolation and inbreeding, the sheep here are below normal size.

The slope was so steep and the rock so loose that I had great difficulty in taking off his skin and keeping the carcass from falling. While I was doing so, the flies increased to incredible numbers. I have never experienced anything like it. They covered me and the ram. At last the skin was off. I found his stomach full of food, much *Ephedra* in it and other leaves and stalks. His bladder contained almost no liquid and was shrunk to two inches. The sheep of this mountain have thus adapted themselves to living without water except for such as can be obtained from their food. They don't even have recourse to the juices of cactus.

I cut off the whole hindquarters, took a good quantity of stomach contents for study by the botanists in Washington, put the skin and horns in my rucksack, drank up the rest of my water, shouldered all, and struggled down to the foot of the mountain. In doing so, owing to the load, the soles of my shoes were completely torn off. I cannot forget the misery of my struggle under the load, more than three miles around the mountain, across the sandy desert to camp. It was at the period of the day's greatest heat and my suffering was intense. On reaching camp I was pretty near a state of exhaustion. Throwing off the load, I poured out the cool water from the desert water bag. My thirst was not satisfied until I had drunk two quarts. Then I made a cup of tea which seemed to invigorate me. A rest restored my strength as the shadow of the mountain extended to include my camp.

I salted and put away the hide. Then I cooked supper. It was dark when I finished eating it. The moon was half full, the heavens brilliant, a cooling breeze was blowing. I went a short distance from camp and stretched myself flat on my back with the firmament spread out above me. With delicious contentment I lay there for two hours, giving myself up to thoughts of my dear Louisa and the little ones. Then I wrote these notes of the events of this day—one that has brought a reward for all the work and risks undertaken. Never before have I earned more fairly the trophy now in camp—a trophy only until I reach Wellton, from where it will be shipped to the Biological Survey for the interest of science.

March 11. Insufferably hot, no breeze. Until yesterday, a strong wind blew continually from the north, night and day. It was a hot wind, yet when I was climbing a mountain and perspiring it cooled me. The wind now seems to have stopped. In the morning I took a much needed rest about camp and cared for the skin and skull. In the afternoon I walked south, halfway around the base of the main mountain, going close to the slopes and carefully examining for signs of sheep, but saw only very small old tracks, none fresh. I found a verdin's nest in an ironwood tree close to camp. It contained five eggs.

Houseflies swarm about camp. My buckskin shirt, now somewhat tainted with mutton from bringing in the meat, attracted a swarm to me all day and they were almost intolerable. Biting flies were equally as abundant and I have never suf-

North section of the Sierra del Rosario as seen from the crest of the central section.
Charles Sheldon.

fered more from insects. Where these flies breed in this dry
country I know not. The flies made a perpetual hum about camp
all day. At dark all the flies retired and the relief is a satisfaction.
I shall never again attempt desert hunting so late as March. But
the nights are balmy and deliciously cool. I sleep with but a canvas over me.

The El Rosario mountain consists of three main sections: the
central, which is about three miles long; the south, about 2 miles
long; and the north, which is 2 miles long. Ridges, partly buried
in sand and discontinuous, extend north for four or five miles
more. Some of these ridges just east of the north section are completely buried in sand. A few sand-buried ridges are on the
extreme south. Sand dunes extend to the mountain base all
along the south end.

The gap between the central section of the mountain and
the south section is half a mile wide at the east end, but at the
west end is narrowed by a ridge of rocky peaks. The gap between
the central and north sections is less than half a mile wide.
There is flat desert in the gaps.

The central or main section of the mountain is the largest
and its highest peaks are grouped toward the south end. My
barometer makes them about 1,500 feet above this camp. There
are six or seven peaks of about the same altitude. All El Rosario
closely resembles the Gila range and is of the same geologic

Huge, odd-looking slabs of rock 200 yards from the western base of Sierra del Rosario. The origin of these boulders still puzzles visitors. Charles Sheldon.

formation. But it contains no long canyons penetrating into it. It is a very narrow range, not more than a mile and a half between the extremities of the longest spurs east and west. It is wider at the south ends of all three sections. The spurs are numerous and all very short, rapidly descending with the slope of the mountain. At intervals of ¼ to ½ mile the side spurs extend out a little farther and enclose small flat valleys. There are only two or three real canyons in the range and these are short and rapidly ascending. The whole crestline is ragged and one cannot travel along it except here and there for short distances. The same is true of the spur crestlines. The mountain extends in a northwesterly-southeasterly direction.

This mountain is rougher than the Gilas for some reason — perhaps it is more exposed to the winds on all sides. Its slopes are very abrupt and all the surface is honeycombed and irregular, and the rock all shattered and wind-worn on the outside exposures. The slopes and crest are breaking away, with shattered masses of freshly broken rock lying everywhere. The furrows

An old Indian trail skirts the east base of Sierra del Rosario. Charles Sheldon.

down the slopes are innumerable and very precipitous, therefore the erosion is very rapid. This mountain is so exposed to the wind that erosion from this cause is very marked. The great boulders lying at a distance from the mountain look as if they were deposited there by ice. Many of the peaks are very sharp and spired. Most of the rock is loose and this causes great danger in climbing. Sand dunes surround the mountain in a belt half a mile out from its base. The dunes are right against the mountains at the north and south ends.

There is practically no cactus here. I have only seen six or seven little stunted *Opuntias*, all on the flat close to the mountain. One *Opuntia bigelovii* [teddybear cholla] is on the slopes. A small sahuaro stands alone half a mile to the east of the south end of the central section. Ironwood trees are abundant along all the washes, but there are no palo verde trees except a few along the biggest washes. The yucca covers the mountains everywhere. A few ocotillos are about and are even on the slopes. *Ephedra* is common all over the mountains and provides the principal food of the sheep. Galleta grass also is abundant on the mountains. Greasewood invades clear to the top, yet it is scarce on the mountain. *Encelia* is common all over the slopes, also *Gaertneria* [bursage], *Elaphrium*, and many other shrubs and plants. Yet, vegetation is scarce as compared with other desert mountains, except for the yucca, more abundant here than elsewhere.

There is no water on any part of the mountains. I have been above every canyon and furrowed slope, and up many of them, and have examined many spurs and have seen no sign of a trail indicating water. I noticed a few depressions in the granite which would hold water, but only for a few days after a rain. An old Indian trail, well preserved and clear, here and there branching and coming together, passed along the east side of the mountain, going through the south gap directly to the sand. This trail goes straight through and not once does it branch off toward the mountain indicating water. It passed close to some points of the mountain. I have found pieces of old broken pottery along it. It is impressive to see this old trail still so clear and realize how much it must have been used many years ago before it was abandoned by the Sand Papagos. It probably was used by the Indians as a route to Laguna Prieta or the salt water, the Indians choosing the route close to the mountains because of the hard ground and excellent walking. I have been over the whole trail along the mountains and could not observe that the Indians ever loitered here except to camp for a night.

I have seen no signs of the chuck-walla lizard. Lizards are abundant (small ones) but scarce as compared with other desert ranges to the east of here. There are no mosquitoes. The nearest water is the Tinajas Altas, 20 miles away, and Laguna Prieta, 25 or more miles. How near the water is out in the sands to the southwest I know not, but it is a good distance. All bird life is scarcer than in other desert ranges, the Costa hummingbird being the most common. I have seen no sign of a golden eagle, and only two ravens and three vultures. Hawks are common, also the nighthawk. The small animal life in the washes is not as abundant as elsewhere and coyotes are scarce. This is surely the most arid mountain, the most destitute of life and vegetation in this whole region of northern Sonora. It contains the most western sheep in Sonora.

Again tonight I lay out on the flat in the cooling air and will sleep there.

March 12. The same heat. At daylight I was off for the extreme north mountain. On the way I found a Costa hummingbird's nest in a small palo verde with two young about half grown. All about these mountains on the flats are numerous badger holes. I have not before seen them so abundant. All the greasewood is in full bloom and very lovely, giving a cheer to this desolation. Most of the *Encelia* has passed bloom and has nothing but dry stalks, yet, here and there, some of it blooms. It is rare that another flower of any kind is seen, except the red flowers on which the hummingbirds feed that are now in full bloom on the abundant shrub along the washes.

I found that the crest of the north mountain is not so rough, but still dangerous. I climbed through the sand at the S.W. corner and reached the crest and followed it north to the low saddle connecting it to another mountain, and then climbed over the crest of that one. The slopes of these mountains are as rough as elsewhere and the crest nearly so. I saw no fresh signs of sheep, only old dung—very old—and all indications showed that few sheep exist in all this range. I found that the ewe and lamb whose tracks were seen at the north end of the main mountain did not cross the gap to this one as I had supposed. I found a fine cave just under the crest and lay in it, protected from the sun, for two hours. Sheep dung was in the cave.

Late in the p.m. I came off the mountain and returned to camp by moonlight. There are no sheep on this north section now. All around these mountains is an old faint trail just above the base. It was undoubtedly made by antelope which must have existed here at one time. Just before dark I saw many night-hawks flying about. They are very abundant here, as are the owls which keep hooting all about at dusk and after. In some places on the south end of the north section the sand has covered the slope for fifty or a hundred feet. Far above this solid sand I found sand scattered about the crevices and irregularities of the slope. It must take hundreds or thousands of years for so much to accumulate.

At about 10 p.m. Win and Staley came with the horses. Tomorrow I leave for Tinajas Altas and then back to Wellton as quickly as possible. It has been a hard trip, but successful after all. The heat has been trying, yet I have tramped just as hard as ever.

March 13. In the morning we made an early start and crossed the sand belt, which is about six miles wide, and on reaching the wagon, lunched. We then traveled through the Gila range to Tinajas Altas, covering 20 miles in about seven hours. This is the nearest water to Rosario. When out on the sand I could see the whole Rosario range. It is approximately twelve miles long, but contains only about five miles of actually high, rugged crestlines. Coming across the Lechuguilla Desert, I collected the large bulb of the scarce *Peniocereus greggii* cactus [night-blooming cereus]. After again passing through the Gilas, I must say that, as to roughness, El Rosario is very similar to the Gila range.

Upon reaching the Gilas [Tinajas Altas Mountains], I found that birds and vegetation at once became more plentiful. Staley had found three fine, large bleached skulls of big rams right here near the Tinajas Altas. They were undoubtedly shot by those

Conference near Tinajas Altas. Left to right, the Chappel brothers, Win Proebstel, and Staley Hovatter. Charles Sheldon.

miserable fellows who come here in summer and watch the water hole. Thus I have the chance to compare the skull of my Rosario ram and find it very much smaller and presenting many different characters. The sheep of Rosario are small and dwarfed, and this fact should be recognized, whatever the cause, by giving them a specific or subspecific name.

My trip is now over and my only task is to get back. It has been very hard, but more than worthwhile, for I have added an interesting fact to science—the changes wrought in sheep by isolation, lack of water, and long inbreeding.

March 14. This morning we packed and had just started when a Ford motor arrived with Jim Chappel and his brother bringing me a telegram which Nelson had sent to Bob Gale, Wellton postmaster, asking him to send out a special messenger to notify me of the condition on the border. U.S. troops were about to cross over and punish [Pancho] Villa for his raid on Columbus [New Mexico]. This was an unnecessary thing on Nelson's part, to undertake to send orders to protect me, etc. I took the motor back to Wellton.

March 15. Win arrived. He and Staley visited the red-tailed hawk's nest from which he had taken two eggs March 3rd and found that it had been deserted. The same afternoon I left on the train.

March 16. This morning I arrived in El Paso which was in the center of the whole Mexican trouble. I discussed the situation with all my Mexican friends.

March 17. I went over to Juarez. Except for soldiers in the streets of El Paso, there was no indication of excitement in either El Paso or Juarez, nor would one have believed there had been trouble.

March 20. I reached New York.

5

A JOURNEY TO SERILAND,
SONORA, 1921–1922

When the open-warfare phase of the Mexican Revolution mercifully came to an end in 1920, Charles Sheldon was able to revive his plans to collect mountain sheep in Sonora's Sierra Seri—the southernmost sheep to be found on the Mexican mainland. Sheldon also hoped to be able to visit fabled Isla Tiburón, a 467-square-mile island located just offshore from the Sierra Seri in the Gulf of California. Here he hoped to obtain specimens of the island's isolated population of mule deer, locally known as bura. The problem was that both the Sierra Seri and Tiburón were the stronghold of the Seri Indians, and the tribe still maintained its traditional ways beyond the reach of Mexican law. Two other explorers, R. E. L. Robinson and James Logan, had been killed by Seri Indians while hunting mule deer on Tiburón Island in 1894, and visiting Seriland was not without risk.

In preparation for his trip, Charles Sheldon read W. J. McGee's monograph on the Seris published by the Bureau of American Ethnology in 1898. In 1894, while surveying Papago settlements in Sonora, McGee encountered a group of Seris camped at Rancho Costa Rica, 40 miles west of Hermosillo. After allowing themselves to be interviewed for a day and a half, the Seris disappeared into the desert. Intending to study the Indians in more detail, McGee returned to Sonora the following year. Unfortunately, recent trouble between the Seris and Mexican ranchers had caused the Indians to go into hiding. Although McGee's party searched the Sierra Seri and Tiburón Island, not a Seri was seen. Willard Johnson, cartographer for the McGee expedition, made a map of the region that was later used by Sheldon. Picacho Johnson, the highest peak in the Sierra Seri, is named for him.

Sheldon arrived by train in Hermosillo, the capital of Sonora, in late November 1921. Now fifty-four years of age, Sheldon was still a rugged hiker as well as an experienced big-game hunter. His expedition was an unqualified success. Although he was not the first American to hunt mule deer in Seriland (W. J. McGee collected a bura buck in the Sierra Seri for the

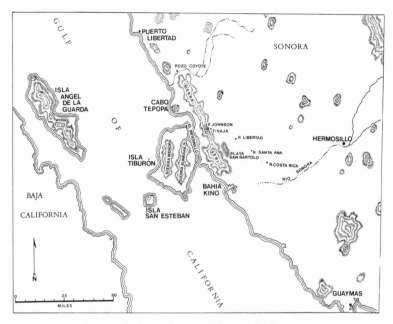

Western Sonara showing the Sierra Seri and Tiburón Island.

National Museum in 1895), Sheldon collected the first bighorn sheep and white-tailed deer in the Sierra Seri. And, although H. E. Anthony had collected a number of mammals on Tiburón for the American Museum of Natural History in 1911, Sheldon was the first to obtain a series of the island's mule deer. What makes Sheldon's expedition truly remarkable, however, is that he was the first and only American to hunt with the Seris on Tiburón Island when these Indians were still living in an unacculturated state. Sheldon's unprecedented lengthy stay with the Indians and his sympathetic and open-minded attitude toward them resulted in observations that are an invaluable contribution to Seri ethnology.

Dec. 1, 1921, Thursday. I had intended to start from Hermosillo yesterday, but my chief man, Chapo Campos, did not appear. He was found late in the day, drunk. I had rented four mules and two horses and had them brought to Hermosillo last Sunday from Morgan's ranch, thirty miles out. I had also employed a vaquero, Pablo Vega, to come along, as he claims to know the country. I had to have pack saddles made—one can get nothing in Mexico during these times. Finding that I could not start, and having lost confidence in Chapo, I sent Pablo ahead with the stock to the Costa Rica Ranch. This morning I employed a motor, loaded in all my equipment, and after motoring 43 miles reached the ranch. Pablo arrived with the horses soon after. The ranch is owned by Jim Blevins who bought it from the Encinas heirs.

The country is flat all the way to the ranch. For sixteen miles there are many small ranches along the road, nearly all occupied by those who cut and haul wood to Hermosillo. The grazing is good for fifteen miles out but there is no stock. The rest of the way is not interesting, only greasewood [creosote bush] and some cholla cactus. Two or three small ranches were passed but they were of no account. I saw several jack rabbits (*Lepus alleni*) [antelope jackrabbits], mostly in the cholla. I shot two and took their skins.

At Blevins' I had a lunch of venison, beans, and tea. He arranged for a Papago Indian, Antonio Castillo, to go with me, and I got an extra horse from him. I passed the night sleeping on a dirt floor.

Pablo Vega (left) and Antonio Castillo packing a mule. Charles Sheldon.

Dec. 2. With the usual delays, we got the animals packed and we started at 10:30 a.m. Then my troubles began. The mules were not accustomed to packing, the pack saddles did not fit, and at once two bucked off their packs. Then, since the latigos and sling ropes were short, and Pablo knew little about packing and Antonio nothing, every two or three hundred yards a pack would be bucked off or fall off and progress was painfully slow.

The country is flat all the way to the Santa Ana Ranch, which we reached at five p.m., fifteen miles from Costa Rica. The country is full of giant cactus, organ pipes, and cholla growing in a dense chaparral of ironwood and mesquite trees, now and then a palo verde. There is scarcely any grass and it is more like a thin forest than a desert. A few jack rabbits were seen, very few birds—Gila woodpeckers the most abundant, also vultures, a few phainopeplas and flycatchers, including a vermilion flycatcher.

At the ranch we found that all the mules had sore backs and we could not make the trip with the pack saddles. Pablo started off to see if we could get a cart and harness at a ranch 3 miles

A *malacate* (a winch for hoisting water from a well) at Rancho Santa Ana. Charles Sheldon.

distant. I was sleeping when he returned not having been able to find the ranch. It is very discouraging. If a wagon cannot be obtained I must return to Hermosillo and get one.

At Santa Ana the method of getting water from a well 90 feet deep is primitive. A large wheel 20 feet in diameter is placed horizontally on a frame and a rope wound around it. The wheel is revolved by a mule which is hitched to a beam inclined from the wheel. Thus a bucket made of a cowskin is lowered to the water and then raised. They keep this going all day and late into the night to lift water for the stock. This wheel is called a *malacate.*

The stock is mostly horses. They have a few cattle for milking to make cheese. There are four or five hundred horses running wild, belonging mostly to Blevins. These horses come in every night to water and one hears the tramp of hoofs, running or trotting, all night long. There is very little grass in the whole country, yet a thousand head of cattle, perhaps more, could be grazed. There are now only a few.

Dec. 3. This morning Pablo and I, driving the mules ahead, rode to San Isidro Ranch and found that we could get a cart. Ybarra, the owner of the cart, and his active, pretty wife were most hospitable and assisted and fed us. Ybarra's ranch is called Palo

Santo Blanco and his family at Rancho Libertad. Charles Sheldon.

Alto. Pablo drove the cart back and brought our material, arriving after dark. We slept on the ground outside. The horse I got at Costa Rica disappeared in the night and I decided to go on without it.

Ybarra has about 15 horses and 30 milk cows. All is sand and chaparral about the ranch. There is a well near the corral and water is obtained by hauling it up with a horse. Two small boys provide all the help at this ranch.

Dec. 4. After the usual delays, we started at 11 a.m., Pablo driving, and after four hours arrived at Rancho la Libertad, 12 miles distant. The mules are old and he could scarcely make them go. The country is dreary, nearly all level *playas* [dry lakes], a little cactus. The chaparral has been left behind. En route to Libertad I saw over 20 caracaras [large birds of prey] sitting close together in trees and on the ground. I noticed that caracaras were abundant in the playas, also jack rabbits. For two days I have been seeing the Seri range ahead and long to get there if ever I can.

La Libertad is most interesting. It is the last ranch on our route. There is a malacate and large corrals. About 40 cattle range out through the country and they have 40 cows for milking and making cheese. The ground is very arid and the chaparral is again dense. There are several families here. They live a

Burro Alazán and his wife gathering firewood at Rancho Libertad. Charles Sheldon.

camping life and have only a bare existence, yet we got eggs and good food. The people are most hospitable.

Four families of Seri Indians are camped here. They are in rags and appear most primitive and have wild, fierce faces. The chief, Burro Alazán, told me that there are no sheep on Tiburón Island, but a few in the Seri range. In the evening they came to my camp and danced. One sat on the ground and tapped a canteen in rapid 4/4 time, chanting in monotonous tones, but at times melodic. Another, with rattles wound about the ankles, danced a peculiar jig in unison with the singing, making the rattles sound in perfect time. He held a staff on the ground while shaking his feet. They kept it up a long time and then two others danced. It was a strange sight, with the Mexicans sitting around the fire and urging them on.

It is doubtful if there is water in the tanks of Sierra Seri, thirty miles distant, and I offered a Seri a dollar (two pesos Mexican) to go and see tomorrow. He accepted. Again I am worried. If there is no water I don't know how I can hunt there, especially with such inefficient men as I have, but I must try to make do with the water bags.

Chapo and Romero, Seri men. Charles Sheldon.

Dec. 5. This morning it began to rain. That means I cannot leave for a day or two as the ground will be muddy. At this ranch there are three families. Cruz Zamora and his wife, Maria, give us our meals. I spent most of the time in the Seri camp just outside of the ranch house.

Dec. 6. It rained most of the day and cleared in the p.m. The Seri has not returned yet, but it is certain there is water in the tinajas after this rain. I tried to photograph the Seris but the light was poor. In the evening the Seris danced a long time, one after the other taking the stand, Santo Blanco singing. It was a strange sight around the small campfire. I sleep just outside the building among dogs, pigs, and chickens.

Dec. 7. Beautiful clear morning. I went to the Seri camp early. The chief, Burro Alazán, told me that they were all leaving for Tiburón Island and that after I had killed sheep, if I came across the mountain to the shore and "made smoke" he would come over and take me to the island. They have no meat there and

The Seris prepare to leave Rancho Libertad. Charles Sheldon.

want me to kill some deer for them. I hope to go, in spite of the advice of all the Mexicans to the contrary. They say that once the Seris get me there in their own land they will be very different and at least will rob me of everything. Should they find any cactus fruit so that they can brew a drink which makes them drunk, they may harm me. I will decide after I have tried to get sheep, which the Seris say exist in small numbers in the Seri range. Their name for sheep is "mokwet." More about the Seris later. I photographed them as they were leaving. Romero, the Seri, returned early and said the tanks were full of water.

I changed to a lighter wagon. When shall I ever reach the sierra only 30 miles away in plain sight across the flats? My patience has returned. Now I know I cannot get back home by Xmas. Pablo's father, Don Antonio Vega, came to the ranch at 1 p.m. and will come with us.

We started at two p.m. and went about eight miles across a flat, washed playa. Palo verdes became abundant, part of a dense chaparral of mesquite, ironwood, pitahaya [organpipe cactus], sahueso [also called cardón, this is a large columnar cactus similar in appearance to the saguaro], sahuaro, chamiso [saltbush], brittle bush, and ocotillo. Jack rabbits are numerous and I saw a cottontail or two and a few birds—Gila woodpeckers are the most common and there are a few flickers. I saw three or four tracks of mule deer and one of peccary.

A large sahueso *cactus near the Sierra Seri. Charles Sheldon.*

We camped at dark a couple of miles inside of Sierra Anacoreto. There is no water and only palo verde to feed the horses. The mules gave out and I am doubtful if we can reach the tank. Romero, the Seri, came with us. I think the chief sent him to watch me to be sure of what I am doing. It is most interesting to observe him.

At last I have left human abodes behind and feel the charm

of the lonely desert. It is quite different from that farther north and more fascinating in a way, because of the chaparral. Sierra Seri is ahead and how I long to reach it—if only the mules will last long enough to get us there.

Dec. 8. We rose long before dawn, ate tortillas with coffee, and started. The mules went still slower! Antonio led, I followed, and then the mules, Romero, the Seri, walking beside them and continually whipping them—I was glad to be ahead so that I could not see it. We traveled through dense chaparral over soft ground, always gently rising. Jack rabbits skipped away and I saw a flock of Gambel quail and a variety of birds.

At noon we unharnessed, drank coffee, ate the last tortillas, and then started again. Pablo's father, Don Antonio, caught us—he is a fine old type of ranchero. The grade was steeper. At four we saw five blacktails run away a hundred yards to the left. Tracks were more plentiful. The mules were about finished and we camped and made a little bread. Romero and I started off to look for deer. There were plenty of tracks, some fresh, but we saw no deer. We saw plenty of peccary tracks and a lion's track in an arroyo. We have only made 18 miles in two days but we are near the range. Coyotes were yelling nearby all night.

Dec. 9. At daylight I started and circled around to hunt deer and find the tinaja, allowing the mules to get there as best they might. I walked to the mountain and saw plenty of blacktail tracks, and when higher, whitetail tracks, but no animals. Blacktails were not in evidence near the sierra. I climbed over the foothills and finally found the tinaja, but it was four p.m. and nobody had arrived. I had only taken a cup of coffee in the morning. I went to the water and soon Don Antonio rode up, having ridden far ahead of the mules. He saw a whitetail on the mountainside and I climbed to the top for it but could not find it in the dense chaparral which covers all the lower mountain. Then coming back to camp I found the mules there. After taking a bite I went below for deer, saw none, and returned long after dark. At least we are here.

Dec. 10. At daylight I started climbing the sierra. It is astonishing not to find any sign of sheep or deer near the water. I saw great flocks of doves. The way up the mountain was through dense chaparral and cactus. Reaching a saddle, I climbed a mountain and then saw to the west the sea—the Infiernillo Strait—and Tiburón Island, and to the east the chaparral, and to the south Picacho Johnson—called "Estaku" by the Seris. After walking along and noticing a few deer tracks but no signs of sheep, I sat and scrutinized a range opposite for a long time through my glasses, a range topped by bold craggy precipices above the chaparral which covers the slopes. A movement caught my eye and a fine ram was seen jumping down from the rocks into the brush, where he fed, apparently without suspicion or watchfulness. The only method of getting him was to circle two miles around the connecting ridge and then work downward.

Marking well the spot, I started and worked along below the ridge crest through cactus and brush, every now and then going above on the skyline to look but did not see him again.

Finally I was near the spot and step by step worked down. When within 150 yards above the canyon where the ram had last been seen feeding, I sat down and watched and listened, knowing that if he should appear while I was descending a precipice he would hear and see me. It was very beautiful all about as seen from the upper world. The dense chaparral stretching away to the sea was below me, and to the west the sand beaches of both the mainland and Tiburón were clearly visible. Great precipices were below and the great mountain, Picacho Johnson, was ahead, while to the east were the ranges rising from the vast chaparral of Sonora.

Suddenly the ram walked up on a slight projection of the ridge and stood looking. He was 150 yards away, slightly below. At my shot he cringed and took a tottering step to some rocks and then collapsed and fell below. Not knowing but that others might be about, I waited and watched. Seeing nothing, I continued along the ridge, still looking all about below. When convinced no others were near, I went to the spot and saw him dead just below. He was in a wide canyon and fell down the slope between two spurs. He was a beautiful ram in fine pelage, and though young, he was older than I first thought and his horns were massive.

When I started down to photograph him I found that my rucksack was not on my back—I had left it back at the place where I first saw the ram! I made the toilsome journey back and returned, then made a cup of tea. I photographed the ram from various angles, measured him, and took off his skin. I had to put brush under him while skinning so as to not get the meat dirty. There were ticks in bunches in both ears. In one ear there were over sixty ticks all bunched together. Apparently the ticks had not been in the ears very long as none were swelled.

The shot occurred at 10:40 a.m. but it was nearly dark when I started with the skin and skull and staggered down to camp. Romero was greatly excited on seeing him and at once sang the Seri sheep song, always sung after the killing of a sheep. It was a strange scene around the fire while the Indian sang.

Dec. 11. Early I left for the mountaintop with Romero to show him the meat. He was to guard it against ravens and vultures while Pablo brought up a mule as near as possible to get it. While on top, two whitetail bucks suddenly ran along the mountain slope before I could get a shot. Romero was constantly talking loud, urging me to go to the island, and this frightened the bucks. These whitetails feed and remain above, the blacktails stay below in the chaparral.

After showing him the spot, I left and climbed a very rough mountain and followed the crests and slopes all day. A few signs of ewes were seen but nothing else. These mountains, rough as are all desert mountains, are covered with cactus— *Echinocactus*, pitahaya, nopal [prickly pear], and cholla—and ocotillo, maguey [agave], torote [elephant tree] of three varieties, cat's claw, and a great variety of shrubs. One has to fight this once on the cliffs and rocks. These sheep live and feed in such a country. They browse exclusively. I have never before hunted under such conditions—sheep are most difficult to see. There are evidently but few sheep here and I must soon go alone to another part of the range.

In camp at the tinaja near Picacho Johnson. Left to right, Pablo Vega, Romero (Seri), and Antonio Castillo. Charles Sheldon.

I had wonderful views all day of the sea, Tiburón Island, Angel de la Guarda Island, and the lower California ranges, and to the east the vast chaparral, while Picacho Johnson was almost directly ahead. A few flowers are out. I noticed *Ammospermophilus* [ground squirrels] and two squirrels like gray squirrels [rock squirrels] high up. Hummingbirds, wrens, ravens, flycatchers, mockingbirds, and various other birds were about. Bird life here is abundant. I also noticed a roadrunner high up. I took lunch on the crest. On the mainland shore I saw much smoke made by Seris signaling to others on Tiburón to come over in a boat and take them to the island. The climbing all day was dangerous and there was much cliff work. This is a range that continues directly south of the tinaja.

Don Antonio left this morning. I gave Romero a suit of overalls and a red handkerchief, which delighted him and quite transformed him. Antonio the Papago is a dear fellow but quite useless — too old. The weather here is perfect. Sometimes the sun is hot, but not too hot — not so hot as farther north in the desert.

The nights are not cold and are delightful. I am getting in splendid condition. Tomorrow night I shall camp alone high on the mountain so that I can explore the west side of the range for sheep. I think all the time of my wife and family.

Dec. 12. Today I was disappointed when I thought I had left my first roll of photographs in the Seri camp. I will never see those people again. Later I found it in my chest. I spent the morning preparing the skin and head and cutting the meat into strips — the flies were blowing it. Early in the p.m. I walked up a ridge near camp, but saw nothing but old deer tracks, and then returned. I took my robe and a little food, put it on a mule, and Romero and I went to the top of a high ridge among the mountains south of camp. Here I am at last alone, with a fire in front, looking to the east down a deep wild gorge, the vast chaparral plains ahead, and the mountains beyond seen faintly in the moonlight.

Before making the fire, I hunted about for a deer but saw none. This country in many ways is the most fascinating I have ever experienced in the desert — the game, new scenery, the sea, and the Seri Indians. And what is best, I am probably the first white man who ever made a hunting trip here. Tomorrow I will make a hard long hunt. Crickets chirp loudly all around.

Dec. 13. At daylight I started, climbed the mountain, and finally reached the cliffs. I then circled at their base around on the west side of the high slopes. They are almost perpendicular, completely honeycombed, and covered by a jungle of cactus and thorns like all mountains here. It is almost impossible to see sheep except on the skyline or by coming on one suddenly. I climbed up and down and at times waited, listened, and watched. Before me was the sea, Tiburón Island, and the lower California ranges. Smoke arose from the island.

There are but few signs of sheep, all old, on the west slopes of the mountain. I saw a roadrunner high up, two kinds of hawks, and a golden eagle. I do not see vultures but ravens are common. I can discern a faint sheep trail along the crest of the mountain in some places. Certainly, large numbers of sheep do not travel here. Everything indicates that but few sheep use these ranges.

At noon I lunched on the northwest corner of the range, making tea with beautiful sights before me. Then I traveled west over a connecting saddle to a lower ridge, very broken and rocky, which parallels the big mountain. I climbed a small peak and, while carefully raising my head to look over, I saw ten feet below me the horns (the upper edge of them) of a sheep. I thought it was a ewe. Putting my rifle in position, I slowly rose and saw below me, lying on a crag, a three-year-old ram, completely unsuspicious, alone with the wondrous sight of sea and islands and mountains before him. After looking at him, I scraped my foot. He quickly rose, looked back at me, and jumped over a cliff. I hastened forward, then saw him almost sliding below. When he reached the talus he ran across the slope. He was too small for a specimen so I did not attempt to kill him.

I kept on, around the crestlines, climbing up and down peaks until late, then descended to the chaparral and took the direction toward the mountain where I was camped. While walking along and watching the crestline of a long ridge connecting to the mountain, I saw a sheep on the skyline and my glasses revealed a large ram traveling along. He climbed to the crest and then went along the slope I had been on in the morning. He stopped and fed until it was so dark I could not see him. He was very alert and nervous. I then traveled by moonlight and wound upward, through the jungle, over the steep slopes, and reached camp at nine p.m., thoroughly full of cactus spines. I saw lion tracks in the bed of an arroyo.

I know that if I can reach the spot where I saw the ram very early, he will be there or near there, feeding. But I must go up on the dangerous crest or I cannot see him without scaring him. I shall try, but it is most doubtful if I shall ever see him again. My ambition to go for that ram makes me forget that I am a little tired after a hard day's tramp. The wind roars tonight.

Dec. 14. This morning I rose at 4 a.m. and after a hasty breakfast of tea and puffed rice, started to climb the mountain in the moonlight. Slowly I ascended along the ridge, over the steep slopes and rocks, and through cactus and thorny shrubs, becoming badly lacerated. Finally I arrived at the foot of the broken cliffs, 200 feet high. Here I had to wait an hour for day-light, as it was impossible to climb further by moonlight. At least I felt satisfaction in arriving there early. The crestline of the big mountain is nothing but broken knife-edge cliffs, sheer on both sides for 200 feet, and the slopes below are a jungle.

Finally, when there was sufficient light, I slung my rifle on my back and slowly ascended the crags, fearful that I might find places where no further ascent could be made and I would have to return and try another place. But by winding about I finally reached the top and found it almost as difficult to proceed along as the cliffs. I went along the crest a mile to the point I had care-fully marked when the ram was seen last evening. At last I was approaching the spot. Step by step, without noise, using all my experience, I proceeded, carefully scrutinizing the broken slopes and jungle below for the sight of movement in the brush which was my only chance to detect the ram. Often I sat and listened for some slight noise. Finally I was exactly above and opposite the selected spot. Words can hardly describe the wonder of the scene before me. A ridge of low mountains was below and then the sea. The morning sun cast a rosy glow on the water, Tiburón Island, Angel de la Guarda, and the long line of ranges on the lower California coast. The chaparral stretched to the sea and Picacho Johnson stood up all aglow, with other rugged ranges south of it. To the east were the great expanse of chaparral and other ranges of Sonora. A world of grandeur was around me. There was not a breath of air. The chirping of crickets, the notes of birds, ravens swishing by, and hawks sailing about were the only signs of animal life. Smoke rising from the mainland shore and across on the island signified Seri camps.

I waited, listened, and watched for half an hour. Then, when I was about to rise and advance, my eye caught an indis-tinct line of white behind a palo blanco tree. I looked at it for a moment and saw it move slightly. Then my glasses revealed the ram, browsing on the palo blanco, stern toward me. As near as I could judge, he was 200 yards directly below me, on a badly broken slope falling away almost sheer below the base of the cliff I was on. With rifle ready, I watched him, awaiting a good exposure for a shot. But for a long time the ram kept browsing and moving and did not clearly expose himself in the jungle. I noticed that he was alert and watchful, casting his head up to look around in all directions. Finally a clear shot was offered at his side, and though I tried to aim very low, the bullet went just over his shoulder. He jumped about in confusion and then mounted a high rock and stood there, stern toward me, looking downward and casting his head to the right and left. Then he turned and faced the north, his side clearly exposed. At my shot, aimed at the middle of his left foreleg, he dropped, rolled a few feet against a crag under an *Elaphrium* tree, and died without a struggle. The ram was mine, a fine large one. It was only my long experience and understanding of the habits of sheep that led to my getting him.

I was more than an hour finding a way down the cliffs, and a dangerous way at that, but at last stood by my prize. I photographed him, but could not get good exposures. The ground did not permit measuring more than the front part of him. I could not count all the rings on the horns, but he was over seven years old. The pelage was the same as the other ram, dark and fine. There were ticks in his ears but not so many as in those of the other ram. My bullet had passed through the ram's heart, passing out the opposite side without making a large hole. Then I began the long hard task of skinning him in the hot sun, ravens soaring and flapping around in excitement. Several even sat on rocks not 20 feet away, as if calmly waiting for their feast. At one p.m. the skin was off and the skull sufficiently cleaned. I found among other things the leaves of the palo blanco abundant in his stomach. Then I made a cup of tea and, seated under an *Elaphrium* tree, enjoyed the scenery before me. The Seris call this high mountain "Astemdla." They call the tinaja "Astemdla-go-uk."

I shouldered the heavy load of the skull and skin and started back around the broken slope. I had not gone 20 feet when several ravens flew to the carcass, croaking, as if they had been deliberately waiting for me to leave. It required five hours to reach camp at the tinaja. Pablo brought down my blankets, etc., with a mule. Romero gave a shout of joy when he saw the ram's horns on my back. Then a fine fire and a hearty meal of meat, beans, potatoes, rice, and tea. Then, sitting around the fire, the mountains rising up in the moonlight, Romero sang the Seri song of the successful sheep hunt. Then he was willing to talk.

He says there are 27 Seri families and a few unmarried men. There are only 11 marriageable girls from 12 years up. The men marry them by purchasing them from their fathers. They are very dear and that is the reason why all the men are not married. They must give a rifle, cartridges, knives, or a canoe or a sufficient number of things of that kind to purchase one. When a man wants to marry a girl, he mentions it to her once, then after that, until he can purchase her, they avoid each other. If her family comes to his camp, he avoids her and likewise she avoids him. They have a big feast at the ceremony and that is all. They are strictly monogamous and do not permit consanguineous marriages.

The Seris bury their dead in the ground and leave all of his things there, or, if they do not have them handy, they burn them later. They have one medicine man, a blind man, who lives on the island and is taken care of by his wife. He holds his hands together and looks inside of a person when he is ill and sees the disease, and then gathers herbs and gives them to him. They must pay him well in various things. A few years ago, one Seri had smallpox when on the mainland shore. All the others abandoned him and he went to the mountains, to Picacho Johnson, and was never seen again. But he lives, still sick, and at times they hear him coughing loudly. When I reported hearing a blacktail cough while I was skinning my first ram, Romero said it was this Seri.

They have a powder made of flowers they scatter to make it rain. Most of the men have a little idol carved from *torote* [elephant tree], which is his saint. He takes this to a secret cave in the mountains and goes there and prays in song for what he wants. Apparently the idols represent animals—I could not understand him clearly. Romero said they have no god or myths, but it is doubtful if he understood me clearly. The Seris always cook their meat slightly—they eat fat raw at times. The women have only recently learned to use a needle and sew clothes. They do not attempt to explain thunder, the origin of the sun, or other such natural phenomena.

The moon is brilliant as I write these notes.

Dec. 15. This morning I worked preparing the skins and packing to go off to Picacho Johnson (Estaku) to camp alone. In the p.m. I went north along the slope to look for a mule deer. The signs were few—these deer are more abundant lower down in the chaparral. There were many tracks of whitetails, and just before dark I saw a young buck trotting at a distance, high on a slope. I climbed the ridge, waited and watched, but saw nothing and returned. All the mountains and the plains below are covered more or less by ancient sea shells. Everything is ready for starting tomorrow.

Dec. 16. Early in the morning we started, Pablo riding the white mule, I my horse, and Romero Antonio's horse. We traveled over a Seri trail above the tinaja, not very steep but rough, and went through a pass and descended a narrow valley to the chaparral below. Deer tracks (both kinds) and peccary tracks became abundant. It was a wonderful five-hour ride among the foothills and plains with views of the strait covered with a blanket of clouds close to the water, no wind, all the mountains clear. At one place was an old camp at one time occupied by Seris where, after a rain, water can be obtained by digging in an arroyo. Here I found a small carved canoe and put it on my saddle. We rode to the very foot of the west side of Estaku. I saw a whitetail running away. Then we took the pack mule up a very steep, rocky canyon, well up, and deposited my things under an ironwood tree. We took a water bag and walked up through an almost impenetrable jungle for over a quarter of a mile to where there were two tinajas with ten or fifteen gallons of water in each. Thousands of wasps were floating dead and decaying on the top of the water, which for that reason was putrid and smelled horrible. It is all I have and therefore I must use it.

After filling the water bag, we came back and the men left

me here alone in one of the wildest, roughest, and most wonderful spots I have ever camped in. Behind, Estaku rears up; rugged, rocky mountains envelop me on both sides; ahead is "Aseedna," a beautiful sharp peak; and to the west are the sea, the north end of Tiburón, Angel de la Guarda, and the lower California coast. What a jungle on the mountain slopes!

At 3 p.m. I started and climbed through the jungle on the south slopes to the crags above, finding, I am glad to say, a little water in a tinaja right near camp. After cleaning it out I climbed to the top of the spur and found old sheep dung, but such rough going I do not see how I can find sheep unless I shall have luck. I climbed a considerable way and scrutinized the slopes and skyline until it was late, but saw nothing, and I returned and reached camp by dark. There might have been a dozen sheep near, feeding in the jungle, and I would not have seen them.

I cooked rice and bacon and ate a tortilla. It is absolutely silent here except for crickets. The crickets are fairly making a chorus all around me. The moon is not up and the stars are very bright. The moonlight does not touch this side of the mountain until nearly morning. The mountain outlines are dimly visible. If only I can get another ram!

Dec. 17. Today I ate breakfast in the dark—puffed rice, tortillas, and tea—put a little bag of *pinole* [parched corn] and a quart canteen of water in my rucksack and started climbing a spur to the south. Carefully and noiselessly, I gradually ascended, noticing very old sheep dung. I kept ascending the crest of the spur, scaling peaks and looking for sheep, often sitting and listening. I saw ground squirrels, golden eagles, and hawks, sparrow hawks being particularly abundant. I noticed that they perched on sahuaros high at the heads of canyons and caught the large winged grasshoppers that were abundant. The tops of the sahuaro cactus were white when looking down on them and often shone in the sunlight. This gave a brilliant effect to the background of green below them. This effect is characteristic of the whole region. Another thing characteristic of the mountains here is the palo blanco tree. It lines the crests and its long leaves

A palo blanco ("white stick") tree. Charles Sheldon.

hang downward, producing a delicate fringing effect. This tree, of strong wood, grows abundantly on cliffs and in rough, steep places and affords a welcome handhold when climbing. The Seris use it for poles to carry loads because it is tough. Its white bark, much of it hanging in strips, makes a constant noise in the breezes and winds, and the light color brightens the somber background of green. I found little tinajas of very putrid water here and there. The jungle is thick everywhere.

I reached the main mountain and looked upward at the series of succeeding cliffs. I hesitated for some time, but Estaku, looming up high above, lured me upward and I began to climb. I can never forget scaling cliffs hour after hour, and fighting through the jungle of cactus and thorns, pausing to look and listen for sheep and to view the wonderful landscape below. Sheep signs became more abundant as I went up, but all were old, the dung being last summer's droppings. Once I nearly gave up further ascent, thinking of my wife and family, but at last I was lured on. Back and forth, over rocks and crags I ascended, and at 3:30 p.m. reached the crestline a mile or less to the south of the main peak. Then I moved more rapidly, along the crestline, here and there encountering dangerous crags. Sheep range along the crest in fair numbers in summer I should say.

At 4:30 p.m. I was on the peak with the glorious panorama about me, sea, islands, chaparral, and desert mountains. It was a little hazy and I could not see clearly very far. I did, however, recognize the Pinacates far to the north, and faintly the Tule range beyond. Such a wonderful sweep from this peak, one of the highest in the Sonora coast desert. Unfortunately, the press button of my Kodak was broken and in vain I tried to find the screw to mend it. I could find no record of Johnson's ascent of the peak.

I sat and watched, filled with happiness, until six. Then I ate a little pinole, and gathered as much wood as possible. I built a fire, but the wood was so small that in three or four hours it was gone. I spent a very cold night, shivering and trying to find a little wood in the dark, but the ground was too dangerous to hunt far for it in spite of the moon. I tramped and stamped all night. The moonlight was glorious during the night.

Dec. 18. I was glad to at last see the dawn. I hunted very carefully for a record of Johnson's ascent but could not find it, not even a pile of stones. I wonder if he really reached the top, or spent the night along the ridge? I started early to descend along the north ridge and all the way it was equally dangerous. But I find I have not lost in the least my courage in scaling up and down cliffs. Yet when I descended the last one I was relieved.

Piccacho Blanco or Aseedna, with dense "chaparral" in the foreground. Charles Sheldon.

When halfway down and walking along the rim of a vast deep canyon, very narrow, the side cliffs perpendicular for hundreds of feet, I looked across at a narrow talus slope and saw a very large ram. He was not a hundred and fifty yards away, quietly feeding, not suspecting me in the least. I did not care to kill him as I could not cross the canyon and the ram would surely fall below where it was inaccessible. I had shaken the screw out of my Kodak and repaired it and hoped it was working. I tried a shot at him with the Kodak. At last I tumbled a small piece of rock. The ram had occasionally thrown up his head to watch, but at the sound of the rock he became alert and carefully looked about, and then began to run upward. I kept perfectly still. He did not see me. At last he leaped on a crag, took a long look, and jumped out of sight.

Later in the p.m. I finally reached the northern foot of the mountain, very hungry but still strong. I had found water (bad) and was not thirsty. While walking along a lower ridge, a deer whistled in the jungle not ten feet from me. I did not see it. I fought my way up through the brush in the dark to camp. After eating rice and bacon and drinking a cup of tea, I feel no bad results from the trip. I have not seen a vulture here. The ground squirrels are on the very top. There is a great variety of birds here. This has been a wonderful two days.

Dec. 19. Early this morning I walked down the slope, and reaching the flat, carefully hunted across and upward for deer. I was off for the day to hunt the top of Picacho Blanco (called "Aseedna" by the Seris), a 3,000-foot peak near the sea, stretching north and south for about 2 miles. The slopes are very steep and broken and covered with the jungle. The lower chaparral is full of tracks—whitetail deer, mule deer, peccaries, coyotes, an occasional lion—but one can see but a few feet in any direction.

I arrived on the crest about 11 a.m., well south of the peak. I carefully looked and listened as I went along, but did not see even a sign of sheep. About 12:30 I was near the peak, which shot up in cliffs 200 feet high or more. I decided I could not climb it and thus my day's hunt was ended so far as sheep were concerned. I would go below for deer. As I sat looking across the perpendicular west slopes of the mountain, the sea seemed almost directly below and the plaintive screams of gulls and terns were constant and sounded most alluring. I looked across at a slope of a spur that juts out from the north end of the peak and suddenly saw a yearling ram make a short dash and start to feed. Then a good-sized ewe and a big ram followed. They were even within a very long shot, but I did not fire because I did not think I could recover them. One could not pass around the base of the peak and the only apparent way to approach them was to descend to the foot of the mountain and climb up at the north end. I did not have enough time for this, so I decided to attempt to climb over the peak.

Slinging my rifle, I started. The rock is granite and most of it is loose and very dangerous. I began to work my way up the perpendicular wall, which was as dangerous as anything I have ever attempted. I was halfway up when I found I could not advance further. I descended and tried in another place. More than halfway up I had to give it up and it took a long time to descend.

Then I rested to regain my nerve, and tried in another place. I can never forget the final climb, but at last I reached the top. With the sense of relief came the sobering thought, how would I get down?

The sheep had gone back toward the peak and out of sight before I attempted my climb. But knowing the habits of sheep as I do, I was sure that they were on a point below the north side of the peak. They had been living on the top for some time—the signs were there to show it. Picacho Johnson was to the east, the sea to the west, and the gulls still made music.

I cocked the rifle and step by step advanced, without making any noise, and reached the north side of the peak. Slowly looking over, I saw a ewe, apparently pegged to the wall halfway up a cliff. Gradually raising my head, I saw the ram, a ewe, and two yearling lambs quietly lying down on a crag on the side of the cliff above a canyon which fell away many hundreds of feet below. Beyond was the sea and Tiburón and the screaming gulls. This indeed was a sight! I had them not a hundred feet away, but could not shoot without losing them when they tumbled below into the canyon. The sun prevented a photograph.

Then, after considering a while, I shouted, holding the rifle ready. All arose and began to look around. I remained motionless. Then the lambs, in a series of jumps, went diagonally down the cliff, followed by the ram and ewe. They passed me not fifty feet below, not suspecting where I was. They reached the slope above the canyon and stopped to look. Holding my rifle over the edge of a rock, straight down, I killed the ram, the bullet striking his horn before hitting his back. He was only 200 feet below. The ewe ran across the slope and stood at the edge of a spur. A shot killed her and she dropped over the other side. The lambs ran over a crest and then appeared to the right, standing on the knife-edge of a spur below, looking. It was amazing to see how easily they ran and jumped over the rough, dangerous ground. They finally saw me when I moved and ran out of sight.

Now my problem was to get down this north side of the peak, which was equally dangerous. After three unsuccessful attempts, I succeeded without accident. It was late. The ground was too steep to measure the sheep. I hastened and took the skin off the ram. Then I found the ewe, her fall stopped by brush and cactus below, and took her skin off. It was six p.m., dark in half an hour! I shouldered the skins and heads and started downward. Halfway down it was dark. I cut a staff from a torote tree, not very strong, and step by step worked down, punished by cactus and thorns.

I reached the foot at ten p.m. without accident, then I made a fire and ate pinole. I put the skins up in a palo verde tree and the heads in a sahueso cactus. I could not find a good route through the jungle in the darkness, but I struggled up to camp, reaching it at 1 a.m. I have taken too much risk today. I will not hunt more for sheep. I am now safe and have a good series. I do not feel exhausted, even after a day such as this. Was this my last sheep hunt? More tea and then I slept.

Dec. 20. Rising at daylight, I ate puffed rice, arranged the camp, and started early to hunt deer, hoping to meet Pablo with the horses—he was to return today. I went along the lower slopes of Picacho Blanco and saw numerous deer tracks. Suddenly two deer, whitetails, dashed out from nearby in the jungle. One paused a hundred yards away. A shot in the shoulder killed it. I did not see the other one. Hunting these deer is simply jumping them in the jungle like grouse in Vermont. Walk, walk, walk and if you have luck you get a shot. This was a fine young buck. I shouldered the whole buck and staggered with it half a mile to the tree where I had put the sheep skins. The coyotes had been yelling below all night and I was worried that one might climb the tree and destroy the skins, but they were unharmed.

While I was preparing the skins, Pablo and Romero came along with the horses. When Romero saw the deer and sheep he almost went crazy and begged me to go to the island. When I told him that I would, he jumped about in joy. They went up to my camp and brought back the load, and we lunched under the palo verde tree, eating deer liver. How easy it was to take off the deer's skin with assistance!

We packed the mules, put the meat behind our saddles, and in five hours rode back to our camp at the tinaja. On the way a hawk (not a red-tail) flew up and I found a rattlesnake three feet long that the hawk had killed and half eaten. I noticed that the doves gather in certain places in flocks of 40 or 50 and pass the night, usually in a canyon. They go to the same place night after night. Rosario, a Mexican from Rancho Libertad, had arrived in camp to pass some time and eat an abundance of grub.

Dec. 21. Today I have remained here in camp preparing skins and skulls and packing. After much thought and hesitation, and against the advice of all here with whom I have discussed it, I have decided to go to Tiburón Island alone with the Seri Indians. Romero has been urging me to go and the chief, Burro Alazán, invited me. No white man before has ever attempted such a thing and I shall be the first to see the Seris and their natural life in their home on the island. But mainly I want to kill some of the mule deer on the island. Somehow, I have confidence that I can get along with these savage Indians so as to at least come back alive, though I may lose all I have. I am leaving these notes in my chest, and my final thoughts are those of love for my dear wife and children.

We have little food left, but I shall get along with anything the Seris have if they give me the opportunity. Tomorrow morning I will pack a horse and leave for the coast—I will write the details later. At least I do not feel that I will be taking nearly the risk that I have been when climbing these crags and cliffs. I have had no time to collect small mammals and cannot get the Mexicans to do so. Hunting big game consumes all possible time, at least when it is done alone as I do it.

Dec. 22. This morning we rose long before daylight, ate some breakfast, as usual without spoons, knives, or forks—they had been lost before we reached the Santa Ana Ranch by bucking mules. I packed a mule and we started, I riding the horse, Pablo a mule, and Romero on foot. We brought rice, tea, sugar, some beans, puffed rice, the rations being small. Most of the food is gone, the men having consumed such quantities of it.

We pulled through the pass over the mountain and descended through a canyon to the chaparral below and soon left all the Seri range behind us. Since arriving at camp the stock has had no grass, having subsisted by browsing ironwood, palo verde, and a few other desert plants. They had no strength and gave out, so then Pablo and I divided the pack and walked. We are to make a point marked "X" on the map.

Shortly after arriving in the chaparral, Romero lighted a dead pitahaya to make signal smoke to be seen by the Indians on Tiburón Island so that they would come over and meet us in a canoe. As we went along he continued to light these fires for smoke signals to mark our course. He seemed surprised that there were no smoke answers from the island.

After five hours of traveling we reached the sand point from which we are to embark. Then he made a big smoke. Soon, off to the southeast, ten miles back on the mainland, smoke arose and Romero said the Indians had been recently in that direction and that this signified that they were returning to their only canoe at a place ten miles south from here along the beach. Soon a mile in that direction another smoke arose and he started on a trot to make the ten miles and ask the Indians to come and get us in the morning. After a cup of coffee, Pablo left and I am alone.

There are no less than five smokes marking the course of the Indians toward their canoe. It is strange and delightful to be sitting here in mild, calm weather, pelicans flying by, other birds flying back and forth in hundreds along the continuous sand beach, the whole Seri Range behind, and Tiburón Island with its mountains looming up ahead across the strait. I can look back and see the smokes marking our course of this morning and watch the smokes of the Seris as they advance, while Romero is on the run along the beach to meet them.

Mule deer tracks have been abundant, even on the beaches, also coyote tracks. Numerous willets, very tame, were feeding on the shore, also two or three herons, one a great blue. The chaparral grows less dense within a mile of the beach.

I am now wholly in the hands of the Indians and am interested to see what will happen. Nobody has ever had this experience before. I have nothing with me to give them, not even food, but have a few small gifts in the wagon which I shall give them on my return.

Preparing to depart for Tiburón Island, which can be seen across the strait. Left to right, Romero, Francisco Molina, and Burro Alazán. Charles Sheldon.

Seri Village on the beach on Tiburón Island. Charles Sheldon.

Nine p.m. and Romero has not returned. Just before dark a heavy rain suddenly descended and I and everything are soaked. But I had taken the precaution to go way back in the *monte* and gather plenty of wood. I kept warm by a fire. The rain only lasted half an hour. Now there is nothing to do but attempt to sleep in my robe in great uncertainty as to what is going to happen. My feelings in this camp, with the water absolutely calm and the gulls calling in the dark, are a strange mixture of anxiety and hope.

Dec. 23. It was long before I fell asleep, but finally I did and at 1 a.m. was aroused from sleep by a sound, and lifting my head saw a human figure creeping across the sand toward me. The sound was a low voice. I had my rifle under the robe and drew it out before I sat up and said, "*¿Quien es?*" (Who is it?). Romero arose – this was his method of approaching my camp. He said he had met the Seris and they had taken him to the island. He and the two chiefs, Francisco Molina and Burro Alazán, had just returned to pass the night on the beach and would take me to the island in the morning. This relieved my shock, and quickly rising I met the chiefs coming into camp. Molina had a distinguished appearance. He greeted me with "I am very good man" (in Spanish). Burro Alazán's face was heavily painted and a white dot was on each cheek and the nose. Molina's face was not painted. I greeted then heartily, made tea, and gave them tortillas from my scanty stock. Then, after talking awhile, I went under the robe. They simply lay down by the fire in their thin rags, and at times in the night when there was no fire, I saw them sleeping soundly, and it was cold and the wind blowing. But when it became much colder before daylight, they all rose, built up the fire, and sat about it.

I rose at daylight, made tea, gave them cigarettes, tortillas, and some puffed rice and sugar and milk, which they greatly relished. Then we went to the canoe, a long, heavy old rotten affair like a long dory. They partly filled it with brush and on this put my stuff two feet above the bottom. There were five awkward, clumsy paddles. They pushed off. I took a paddle and at first they began to paddle with great speed. But, having paddled all summer, my condition was good and I kept up without trouble, putting strength into it, and I think they were surprised and pleased. Romero told me that since I had killed four sheep they thought I was a great hunter.

We paddled diagonally for $3\frac{1}{2}$ hours, fully seven miles, to their camp on the sand. Seven or eight Indian children ran along the beach as we approached, and around the curve was the strange-looking camp, a white flag flying and women, children, and Seri men running up to meet us. Most had their faces painted – all the women. As we landed, all surrounded the canoe

A Seri reception party. Charles Sheldon.

and all the women began to laugh. I soon saw they were laugh-
ing at my white arms (my sleeves were up). The women came up
and many felt of my arms. All gathered around me in a circle
and felt of me and continually stared at me. It was a strange,
wild assembly of savage people. They looked at everything I had.
Then some boiled sea turtle meat was brought to Romero, but
nothing offered to me. Dogs were abundant.

Their *jacales* [huts] were grouped on the sand. I simply sat
coolly and in good nature patiently waited. Then one brought
out a deer mask they use for hunting and Romero suggested I
photograph it—I did so. All the girls were continuously running
back to their houses to put on fresh paint, and one had rubbed
off her red paint and came out with rows of white crosses on her
face. I continued to photograph them and even grouped them.
Then, as it was past two, I got the tortillas and boiled water at
the house of Molina and ate them, with all staring at me. Then I
circulated among the houses. All treated me well. Romero shot a
bird (a willet) with a rifle and I took off its skin, which greatly
interested them. The women were all making baskets. Meat of
the big turtle was abundant and the kettles were boiling it and
all were eating at all times.

Soon several men gathered to play with a pack of cards—

A Seri man displays a deer-hunting mask. Charles Sheldon.

gambling. I did a trick or two which greatly mystified them. The two chiefs and several women and girls put up a shelter nearby for me to shield me from the wind on the beach. All treated me kindly. They gave me some turtle meat, which is delicious. The dogs beg, but do not snatch food. I have never been amid such strange and interesting people. All seem very kind toward me and yet Romero stays by my stuff and I notice he continually watches it.

I spent the p.m. among the jacales observing the basket making, the pounding of the shells of green turtles to boil out the fat from it, and the general merriment of all. The card game

145

Seri women. Charles Sheldon.

Burro Alazán with his wife and a group of children. Charles Sheldon.

Burro Alazán and Francisco Molina ready to set out on a deer hunt. Charles Sheldon.

kept going all the time. Romero simply sat over my stuff when I was not there. They gave me some more turtle meat. I notice that all toe out when walking. I cooked some rice and bacon, with nearly all the Indian families sitting around me to watch. All were good natured except one tall young fellow who showed some bravado, but I think perhaps it was his method of showing off.

In the evening all gathered and dancing and singing began. Even children danced. The singer uses a rattle, always in rapid 4/4 time, the rattling continual without intermission, but pauses between different songs. They dance only when the singing is on. The girls kept painting their faces differently every little while. Some of the children are painted. After two hours I went to my camp and they all transferred the dancing there—until 2 a.m. I am very sleepy—more about the Seris later.

Dec. 24. This morning at daylight about 20 Seris gathered about my camp and watched Romero and me eat puffed rice. Of course I had to give a great deal away, also sugar. Then I packed

Burro Alazán and Francisco Molina in camp in the interior of Tiburón Island. The deer-hunting mask (left) was brought on the hunt but not used. Charles Sheldon.

some of my scant food—I only brought enough for two men for a week. Burro and Francisco came to camp without anything but rifles, and about ten we got started on a mule deer hunt, Romero remaining behind to guard my provisions. We got a rat last night in the trap and I skinned it before leaving.

We then started. Burro led, carrying a pack of 80 lbs., I had 60, and Francisco less. They went at a rapid walk in a direction diagonal to the mountains. No stops, no conversation, but just walking, I pausing once to fix a *gaurache* [sandal]. We reached the first mountain in two hours and then encountered much cholla and they had to go slower. Each took off one guarache while climbing, evidently to avoid the slippery bottom of the cowhide. On top they rested long enough to put on the guarache, and then started at the same rapid pace across a chaparral plain and through and over another mountain. After four hours of this very hard, fast tramp we stopped in chaparral, surrounded by sierras, with a fine outlook to the north over the wide interior plain and mountains beyond. Then they spoke for

Francisco Molina with a bura *(mule deer) buck. Charles Sheldon.*

the first time and said, "Camp water near" – a tinaja in the sierra eight miles distant! Such fast, serious traveling under loads I have never seen.

No deer tracks were encountered until we reached the sierras, and then they were somewhat scarce. Francisco took the heavy load to the top of the first sierra, then we made a fire, tea (I have not enough), and ate a tortilla each – the last. And then Francisco said, "Come to hunt." He had thrown torote leaves in the fire, saying, "Come." This was for luck to get meat on the hunt – a Seri custom. He started due south through the sierras at a very rapid walk, and I followed, wondering what the Seri method of hunting would be. We have the deer mask, but he did not bring it. Burro remained behind.

So far, the vegetation is the same as on the mainland, but the chaparral is not so dense and the trees smaller. The sahuesos are very fine, and there is much cholla in the sierras. *Encelia* is very abundant and in full bloom, also another shrub with beautiful blue flowers covers the surface [*Ruellia*]. There are beautiful birds, but not so abundant as on the mainland. Hawks, ravens, a few doves and flycatchers and other birds were seen. The doves are mainly seen singly. They suddenly flush from a tree, making a loud flutter and wing whistle. It is often startling to flush them. I saw a few jack rabbits.

Francisco walked on. It has been intensely interesting to watch these Seris glide rapidly through the chaparral, curving about, always choosing the best route by instinct, and without apparent effort avoiding the cactus. I was trying my best to avoid it, but had to keep stopping to brush it off my feet. Not once did either step on a piece of it. They slip through the brush like a coyote, very rapidly.

We went through a pass, having gone two miles. Francisco pointed to a range four miles ahead and said, "*Allá buros muchos*" (Many mule deer there). It was three p.m. All was downgrade to the sierra. Now deer tracks became more abundant and he instantly recognized every fresh one. In one or two places I noticed the ground tramped in a circle where two bucks had fought. They were rutting. I often observed this on the mainland.

We reached the mountain in an hour and proceeded a short distance along the base. Francisco saw fresh tracks going up through a canyon filled with dense brush. Then I realized that here the mule deer feed in the sierras like the whitetails on the mainland. Soon we were going up the canyon, he stepping noiselessly, and I followed, congratulating myself on my ability to walk equally without noise. He stopped often to look, and climbed the slope to the crest. Francisco proceeded carefully, watching the slopes. It was a typical hunt for sheep, just as I would have conducted it. We proceeded along the crest and out on spurs, all the time using the same caution and carefully watching the slopes below on either side. Before us to the west was the vast interior plain of chaparral between the coast ranges of the island. The views were delightful and often I could see the sea to the southeast.

Francisco showed himself a skilled hunter. He did exactly as I would have done and went slowly and carefully. On the slopes and ridges were deer trails exactly like sheep trails. I was perfectly at home in this method of hunting and kept up my own independent watch. About 5:30 p.m. we were on the end of a spur, high up (eight hundred feet), and after a careful look Francisco asked for my glasses. While he was looking through them, I slipped over the slope to a projection, exactly as I would have done for sheep, to get a look over a part of the slope not visible from where we were. Looking down and ahead about 150 yards, I saw a deer moving. Hastening back, I picked up my rifle, grasped his shoulder, and said, "*Allá veo buro*" (I see a mule deer there), pointing. He followed me, but on reaching the spot the deer was not visible. I advanced a few feet and saw what I thought was a doe and put the rifle up, waiting for a good exposure through the chaparral. He pushed my rifle down, saying, "*Lejos. Que venga mas cerca*" (Far away. Let her come closer). But I beckoned him to keep still and in a moment fired. The deer staggered and lay down. Then I saw a buck walk out, and, aiming, fired and the buck fell. Then a small doe appeared and ran behind a palo verde before I could fire and, before exposing herself, she got out of sight around the slope.

Francisco grabbed my shoulder, saying, "*Muy bueno, muy bueno*" (Very good, very good) and hastened toward the buck, which we could not see. As we neared, the buck arose and with two jumps went over a saddle. I hurried forward and saw the buck slowly walking downward a hundred feet below and shot it in the heart. Francisco was much excited and full of joy. We hastened down, and after photographing it in bad light, I measured it and then took off its skin—a terrible job on a steep slope. He did not help except to hold it—a great assistance. We cut the carcass in two and hung it in a tree. When we hung up the meat I noticed he was not so strong in the arms, nothing like his strength in legs and back and shoulders.

I have not emphasized how greatly excited the Seri was after he saw the game. He trembled and was almost beside himself and not nearly so cautious as before. When I shot and hit the deer he was crazy and his actions were hysterical.

It was almost dark. All this, with the sea in view and also the vast expanse of the interior. We carried the head and skin back up and went to the place where the other deer had lain down, but she was not there. Her trail took a deer path near the crest, circling at the head of a canyon, and here and there blood. I told Francisco to stand at the top of a peak and watch. I would follow and kill her. He reluctantly did so. I followed the track and when I had passed around another slope in a circle I saw the deer, well across the canyon, walking along the slope. Looking up, I saw Francisco throwing his arms about, fearing I would not see her. She was 100 yards away. The shot, in bad light, killed her dead. I saw him hastening down. Reaching the deer, I found it a young buck. We quickly took out his insides and hung him in a tree.

It was dark. Going a short distance below, we made a fire on a steep slope near an ironwood tree. I had only a half a quart of water and three cigarettes. We put liver on the coals and ate it. Then I built another fire and lay between them, and he on the other side of the first. It was cold, but the fires kept me warm enough. The rocks were rough. For a long time I lay with my thoughts on home and dearly loved wife and children. The night before Xmas. Finally I slept and passed the night well, only renewing the fires occasionally. Francisco slept well, but I noticed he kept close to the fire. Yet, I could not have endured the cold side as he did. None of the Seris have blankets. They lie down and sleep by a small fire. I was very thirsty.

Dec. 25. We were up at daylight. After eating more liver, I went up to the deer and skinned it. Francisco had cut a palo blanco crossbar and brought the meat of the other one to the plain below. When he had done so, I had the skin off. Putting skins and skulls in my rucksack, we went down and he took the whole meat of the larger deer and hung it on the crossbar and started climbing over the mountain. I followed, wondering at his strength. Reaching the top and then descending, he pointed and said, "*Ya campo muy cerca*" (Now camp is very near). Looking across the four miles of upgrade plain and brush, and knowing of two miles beyond to camp, six miles in all, I got an idea of the Seri's idea of "very near" when he was carrying more than 100 lbs. of meat! And what was my surprise to see him start ahead on a half dog-trot, and he never stopped, only shifted the load from one shoulder to the other. I had the heads

Loaded with meat, Francisco Molina begins a ten-mile trek to camp. Charles Sheldon.

and skins and it required my walking as fast as I could to keep up with him. Upgrade four miles and not a single stop, and then level for two miles without a stop. Never have I seen such an exhibition of strength. For some distance Francisco dragged a stake along the surface making a line, and finally he dragged it at right angles across an arroyo. This was a marked trail so that Burro Alazán could come back and find the rest of the meat.

We reached camp at 12:30. I drank water, ate puffed rice, and had tea and felt, after all the hard work, splendid. Burro Alazán was away hunting. He soon returned and cut a great slab of meat at once and put it in the fire. He had not eaten, not caring to touch my provisions while I was away. Burro said he had seen nothing, but I noticed the two old cartridges which he had were not on his belt. He had probably fired them at a deer.

Francisco took the water bag and two canteens and started eight miles for water, and Burro went for the rest of the meat. Francisco had dragged a stick a long distance to mark the route. I remained hard at work preparing the skins and skulls. Just before dark both returned. Francisco said he had been on a dog-trot all the way. Both cut a large piece of meat and roasted it on the fire, and then slept at once.

Many places in the chaparral, as in the mountains, I noticed where the buro stags have fought, the ground all getting tramped in a circle. Hummingbirds are abundant. I saw vultures, hawks, and many other birds. Now and then a rabbit skips away.

Thus I spent Xmas day, and most of my thoughts are with love toward my dear family. I so hope it has been a happy day for them.

Dec. 26. We started at daylight, immediately climbing the mountain to the north. Then hour after hour we climbed up and down, around the rough slopes of mountains, faster than I would have done while hunting. The sun was hot. Deer sign was not so numerous as farther south. Finally we climbed a high, rough mountain and passed two miles along the crest. It was 1 p.m. The sun had been very hot. It was indeed a vigorous tramp for six hours. Not a deer had we seen and Francisco said the deer had mostly gone south. I saw a spermophile [ground squirrel], black on the head and shoulders, reddish behind—very different in color from those on the mainland. While looking at Angel de la Guarda Island, Francisco said there were many coyotes, jaguars, and deer on it. No sheep, but plenty of lions. [No large land mammals occur on the island.]

After taking some pinole, we descended in a direction away from camp, reached the chaparral, and took a wide circle. Francisco went almost on a trot. I was always relieved to climb the mountains, as I can do it as well if not better than he can. But not on the plains! I, however, kept up. We approached the foot of a small mountain well out on the plains and a deer ran away in the chaparral. Soon he showed me a lion track. There was sign enough, so we kept on, hour after hour, until we had passed back south of camp and circled along a range. Here numerous deer tracks led up, and we started and gradually ascended. Francisco stopped for a long time on the edge of a canyon while the wind blew from him over into it. Soon a deer whistled. I then ascended to the peak and soon saw a doe just below, but she jumped into the brush before I could shoot. It was almost dark and I took a course down the mountain and reached camp long after Francisco had reached it.

On my arrival at camp, Burro was not here. He came in later with his rifle. He has been hunting north, but got nothing. He should have brought water. This had been a day of tremendous tramping. I am tired, but still strong.

Dec. 27. This morning, before daylight, after I had poured water (about all of it) for tea and oatmeal, they informed me that there was no more water, that Burro had emptied the tinaja. But a quart was left! Yet at daylight we started south and continued on a fast tramp, three hours without a pause.

We circled around a mountain and then started to ascend into a big basin that was steep, rocky, and covered with brush. It was full of deer tracks and many were fresh. The Seri went, I am sure, too fast. He did not pause and look often enough and, besides, although his footsteps were careful, they were continuous and always made a little noise.

When up a considerable distance (I was following behind), Francisco suddenly gesticulated wildly and pointed at dense brush and said he saw two does jumping away. One could not see anything. We remained perfectly still for some time, but the does had sneaked away. Then he clapped his hands, much to my surprise, for it made a loud noise. Immediately we heard a rattling of stones, and behind us on a steep slope a fine buck went trotting upwards and passed over the crest before I could get an exposure in the brush for a shot. We ascended this slope and waited for some time. Finally, Francisco went over to the track and tried to follow it. I waited above. When I saw that he intended to follow on and was passing along the slope below, I signaled that I was going upward.

I started ascending, gradually and carefully, looking as I would for sheep. The way was steep and the stones all loose, and a little noise was made in spite of all my caution. As I finally came on a peak rising above a saddle, I looked up at a higher peak, east above the saddle, the dominating peak of the range. From the point where I was I could see almost the whole island, the strait to the east, and mainland ranges beyond the north shore. Also Isla de Patos, the vast central plain, and ranges along the west coast and other high, rugged peaks to the south. The sun was bright.

Just above a bush, a stunted torote, I saw the ears and neck of a doe looking at me. At least I had gone slowly and carefully enough not to frighten her, although I had attracted her attention. She was 125 yards or more above, and when I saw her the rocks where I was were in such a position I could not get a sitting shot. I carefully crept to the left and found a spot where I could sit. Only her head and neck could be seen above a rock. She was motionless, watching me. I carefully aimed at her neck, and at the report she dropped and disappeared so quickly that I knew she had been killed immediately. Then I went downward along the rim to find the Seri, and after a long time I saw him, half a mile distant, below on the lower crest. I finally attracted his attention and signaled by waving my hat to come up. After he started, I went back and climbed the peak and there was a fine mature doe lying dead, the bullet having shattered the vertebra just below the skull. It was an impressive sight to see her on the high peak with such surrounding scenery.

Here on Tiburón the deer replace the sheep of the mainland and are hunted the same. It is fascinating hunting. On the mainland the mule deer are below in the dense chaparral, the white-tails above on the foothills and slopes, and still above, the sheep.

It was 1 p.m. when the Seri arrived. He at once became greatly excited. He had heard my shot and had even found my empty cartridge on his way up. He patted me and said, "*Bueno, bueno*" (Good, good). The Seri are very bad shots and I know that my shooting had greatly impressed him. Then, after photographing, we took pinole in water, which took the last drop of water we had in camp. Then we skinned the doe—at least I did, as he did not help with the skinning except to hold the animal as I asked him, which was a great assistance. Many ravens flew about. Then Francisco cut a palo blanco crossbar and tied up all the meat. He always traveled with a gunny sack tied with long strips of cowhide cord around his waist, like an apron. He used this to put on the ground to sleep on at night, and the cords to tie meat, if it could be obtained. He always carefully cut off and ate all the fat. When hunting in the mountains with a load, he always rolled up his trousers to the knee.

Then Francisco started down. I took a different direction around the crest to look for more deer, carrying the skin and head in my rucksack. I saw many of the spermophiles—they are certainly new. It was then 4, and camp was ten miles or more distant. Fog began to blow over the mountains. I started descending and was among chaparral and small ridges. Fog became dense and around all the mountains and hills, and I could see but a short distance anywhere. I had taken compass directions and traveled north. It became dark and I had to go slowly. There was not a thing to guide me. I would suddenly come to the foot of a ridge and then circle it and again resume my direction. The camp was splendidly chosen in a spot in the brush protected from wind, and the fire was thoroughly concealed. At ten at night I smelled smoke and took the direction against the wind and soon came into camp.

Francisco and another Seri were placidly sitting at the fire, apparently without any thought of me. They simply nodded as I came in. That morning Burro had ascended the point of a mountain and made smoke and another Seri had come. Burro had taken a load of meat back to the village. No water! My thirst

Time to leave the hunting grounds. Charles Sheldon.

is extreme. I broiled some meat on a stick before the fire, ate it without salt, and went under the robe. Burro will return in the morning with, I hope, some water. The Seris don't seem to mind being without water at all. I could drink gallons if I had it. Thus ends my deer hunting in the heart of Tiburón. I have not time for more and there is no water. It has been romantic.

The Indians don't talk much. Every little while they roast some meat and eat it. Burro has a pack of cigarettes, but he didn't offer any to Francisco. I gave him one occasionally, but I have but few.

Dec. 28. All night there was a dense fog and wind. I woke many times very thirsty. After breakfast I prepared the skin and skull. I have eaten nothing but meat without salt. At 10:30 six Seris, including two boys and Romero, suddenly filed into camp with wild, hungry faces. They brought water. They said not a word but at once cut big pieces of meat and slightly warmed it over the fire. They were hungry and had not eaten today. They swallowed it and seemed like ferocious, hungry wolves. One ate some

An osprey nest in a sahueso on the trail to the Seri village. The shrubs in the foreground are brittlebush. Charles Sheldon.

of the meat raw, and the smallest boy ate some raw meat and stuffed his pocket full. They kept eating and eating, warming meat every little while.

I took a hunt for rabbits, but did not see any. After returning, we packed and all started with their loads—all light. They went single file at a very fast walk, and it was a fine, wild sight to

see these Seris ahead, slipping through the chaparral like a
snake. I had to walk as fast as I could to keep up. I had drunk
too much water. We took a roundabout way and were six hours
returning to the village (called *Armen*). They rested once for a
few moments. They avoided cactus while I could not. One of the
small boys asked to take Romero's load, and this boy staggered
along with 75 lbs., keeping up the pace. They saw everything
edible and seemed like wild men. If one stumbled, the others
laughed and this seems the regular thing. I noticed that each
continually inserted his guaraches in the gravel to fill gravel
between them and the soles of his feet. The guaraches are slippery. It was a strange sight before me as I followed the Seris.
Francisco, the chief, slides along the best. He shows more ability
than the others in every way.

I noticed several fish hawk nests in sahuesos and photographed one. The fish hawks are nesting and some of them have
eggs—I saw the birds sitting. They cried when we came near.

As we approached Armen, the Seris single file ahead, numbers of dogs came running to meet us, and then the whole people
came running out, little naked boys ahead. It was a strange
sight. I found the camp hungry, all the food gone. Now how differently they treated me. All shook my hand, women and men
accompanied me to my shelter, they brought water, young girls
washed my dishes in the sea, and two brought new brush to protect me from the wind. I had been the meat provider. It is seldom
that a Seri kills a deer and it is a great event. All begged me to
stay and go hunting in the mountains to the south, a little-seen
district where deer are more plentiful. I felt all were so friendly
and took an interest in me.

After I had eaten some puffed rice, it began to get dark and
they came and told me they were to celebrate with the buro
(mule deer) dance. I went to the group of houses, a big fire in the
center of the group, little fires in all the jacales. All were there.
Most of the little boys were naked and it was very cold. I saw an
old woman lying by a fire, her back naked and only a light mus-
lin cloth held in front. All had eaten meat. They brought out a
dry deer hide, and the son of Francisco put on the deer mask
and held two rattles in his hands. An old man sat before him

with a large rattle and chanted the buro song, and the fellow bent forward and moved his head back and forth sideways and bent down and danced, his feet keeping the 4/4 rhythm. I sat at the edge of Burro's house, naked children sitting against me. It was a strange sight indeed, with wild faces all around in the fire-light. All the Indians seemed to get somewhat excited during the dance and I could see many signs of ferocious natures. A timid person might, in my place, have been a little frightened.

The dancer finally faced me, the song became more rapid, little boys kept time stamping, many chanted, and this was kept up in varying degrees for an hour. I have never been in such strange surroundings, with such a sense of mingling with wild men. Then girls came out and danced and a little boy took the stick. This old man seems to train the little boys every night.

About 12 midnight came another feast of meat. They have no idea of conserving it. They all begged me to go hunting again. They accompanied me to my camp, helped place my robe, and about two a.m. I slept. I have no time to write many notes.

Dec. 29. Early before daylight I was up. The Seris gathered as I ate some rolled oats. I had to give each a mouthful. They continually surrounded me. Then I went off with a Seri for a ten-mile tramp for rabbits, but saw none. But no less than six fish hawk nests in sahuesos were seen—very picturesque. I saw fish hawks carrying sticks to their nests, and some sitting. I did not have my Kodak with me.

I came back at noon and then went among the Indians, photographing. I can now do anything with them. Francisco informs me that he and Burro and Romero will accompany me to Hermosillo. That is interesting, but it means presents, and I have so little food I don't know what to do. In the p.m. I got some baskets (on promises), necklaces, and a block of material with which they paint their faces red and the basket in which it is made. I notice the chiefs are having their wives braid their hair. A woman fixed up Romero's hair. There will be no food here after my meat is gone, but none do anything about it. They have to go ten miles to get water and five men left this a.m. This bringing water is a burden, but they must camp by the sea for

Francisco Molina's wife grooms his hair with a brush made of twigs. Charles Sheldon.

there is their food supply. Several women are making baskets. They are building a new jacal, and repairing the boat with pitch made from the pitahaya.

I have seen not one thing obscene here. All laugh. The card game goes on every afternoon and one or the other joins it. The women do most of the work and odd jobs and I notice they gather most of the wood. When one walks in the distant chaparral and sierras with these people, he realizes he is with wild men with wild-trained senses, like those of animals. The girls and women continually paint and repaint their faces. This, as far as I can see, is nothing but adornment, like that of our women who paint and powder. Yet, symbolism may be connected with it. Several of the women and young girls are pregnant. They retire and seem to have a sense of modesty in nature's tasks. Some of them strip off clothing to the waist during the middle of the day.

I put the children about me and gave each in turn a lump of sugar. They continually follow me. If I go to my camp, many follow and sit about me and all watch everything I do, such as write. One young girl who has kept about camp, cleaning dishes

A Seri man prepares to go for water, carrying it in large ollas suspended in nets from a shoulder bar. Charles Sheldon.

A woman weaving a basket. Charles Sheldon.

Building a new jacal. Charles Sheldon.

The Seris caulk their boat. Charles Sheldon.

A young Seri woman. Charles Sheldon.

and helping, has put different painted designs on her face no less than five times this morning. The colors are blue, red, and white. Red is the most common among them.

They now treat me not only with interest but with respect. I feel that I could do anything with them. Of course I understand that I must make them feel I am a material advantage to them. Here they come in camp to interrupt my writing (2 p.m.). After

Pedro, a young Seri man about twenty-five years old. Charles Sheldon.

eating a little rice, I took vocabulary from them, the Seris surrounding me amid great merriment at my pronunciation. My Kodak was broken in the shutter and I took it apart and got it to work—perhaps—I do not know. The Seris have already practically consumed the meat. They beg me to stay, but I cannot. Not one has a blanket—all sleep in their thin rags by a small fire. They are nearer animals than any people I have ever seen. By

Seri children play on the beach. Charles Sheldon.

degrees I got them to let me photograph indiscriminately, but I have doubts as to the Kodak.

There is a beautiful view in front, with the Seri range and shore birds and numerous fish hawks catching fish. I have talked with all and drawn figures in the sand, and they insist that but seven mammals exist on the island: cougars (not common), jaguars (rare), coyotes, jack rabbits, mule deer, the rat I have taken, and the spermophile. They insist there are no mice – they probably include mice with the *Neotoma* rats. Rattlesnakes, in season, are common, also horned toads. The vegetation is the same as on the mainland, but smaller and not so dense. *Encelia* is more common. I have seen no grass at all. All Seris have a signature which they draw in the gravel or sand as they travel alone, and when others follow their trail they see the signature and recognize it.

After I cooked some rice for supper (only a little) and it became dark, the whole people came to my fire, bringing wood for the purpose of having a great dance because I was leaving. It was perfectly calm, the heavens clear, the stars reflected in the

167

Seri women with loads of firewood. Charles Sheldon.

water. At a little distance the fires in the group of jacales threw up light and scattered glows. The whole scene was really wonderful as the faces of these wild people were seen by firelight — naked children, women and girls all painted. Then Santo Blanco, the best singer, put a bow across two baskets and either drummed it or scraped it to his singing. A boy with two rattles then danced, bending down and shaking the two rattles in rhythm with the singing. His feet rattled time and he twisted round and round.

Then five girls sang. When they sang, they put their hands over their faces. When one put her hands down for a moment, an older woman jumped up and put her hands back. Their singing was fascinating, at times very melodious. The boy would alternate with dancing, other girls also joining the singing in scarcely audible voices. Then came the turtle dance by the girls, a dance praying for weather suitable (calm and bright) for turtle hunting. The men made a deep ring in the sand and five girls stood side by side in the circle. They raised their skirts, holding them like aprons to fill, and began to sing a very sweet song.

All together they edged continually around the circle and lifted their aprons up and down as if begging to have them filled. The whole thing was sweet and full of charm. They repeated it several times, alternating with the boy's dancing.

Suddenly, Santo thrummed the bowstring and began a fascinating, rhythmic song. The five girls stood up abreast, very close together, holding arms. They presented a straight line, then they swayed forward six feet in perfect time with the strange song, and at the right time, backward. The song continued in varying cadences and the well-kept line moved backward and forward in perfect accord, with grace and ease. Their faces could not clearly be seen. The ragged clothes could not either, and the skirts seemed graceful and lovely in the firelight. This dance had wonderful refinement and charm and grace. I have never seen anything quite so wonderful and charming, and there was a refinement about the whole affair which was surprising. I have not seen while here a single thing which is even suggestive of indecency. No civilized community could be more free from it.

The regular dancing by various girls, women, and men continued, and between each dance the girls sang. All the songs seemed different and they seemed to be not only in rhythm, but in rhyme. The whole affair was as romantic as possible and I can never forget it. All the women and men help me and watch every opportunity to do so. It was 2 a.m. when I went under the robe.

The Seris are hungry tonight. They have no food and the weather is not right for hunting it in the sea. The children, the very young ones, still cry in hunger. The little boys, girls, and older people do not seem to pay any attention to it.

Just before dark a Seri with flying hair waded well out with a spear, looking down in the water for crabs. It was a particularly suggestive Seri sight to see this lone wild fisherman out there in the water, with the background and view across the strait.

Three of the Seri, young boys, have a reddish tinge to their hair. All the men, women, and children have their teeth set in a straight line like an ape. Their teeth are white, clean, and worn by tearing meat and bone. I have only six films left. No time to write more.

Seri men line the boat on the mainland shore, and a boy fishes with a spear. Charles Sheldon.

Dec. 30. Before daylight I was up. All the women gathered about the fire as I cooked the last bit of oatmeal. The sugar and everything else is gone—I have given it to them. Then nearly all came and tried in every way to help as we packed up. I said a genuine good-bye and they begged me to stay, but I could not. I gave the children most of my oatmeal and ate very little—I am hungry too. Then they, including girls and children, carried my stuff to the terrible canoe and loaded it on brush put in the bottom. Pedro and I took bow paddles, side by side, a young boy sitting on my feet, Santo and Romero paddling behind, and the two chiefs, Burro and Francisco, behind them. The boat was pushed off. The whole village gathered on the beach, all waving. The boat went forward. My visit to the Seris had ended. After a last look, I bent to work and did not look back again. I felt genuine sorrow to leave them.

The wind was strong, whitecaps danced, and the boat was leaking and very cranky. It took two hours of paddling and bailing to go three miles. I expected to capsize or the boat to break with every roller. I have never felt in more danger, but finally we got across to the regular landing place. Arriving at a sandbar extending out ½ mile, Francisco and Pedro and the boys landed and they pulled the boat along the shore exactly like lining a boat in the North.

Oona (a boy) and another very little boy had spears for crabs. Oona went ahead, watching down in the water, and three times he suddenly pushed his spear (an 18-inch sharp iron spike) in a crab and pulled it out. Then he pierced the crab and killed it instantly.

We landed and sent Santo ahead to make smoke to summon Pablo. Then Francisco said, "My people need meat. Let's go." I took my rifle and we started and walked very rapidly five miles south along the beach, and then struck into the nearby mountains, into a *rinconada,* an intrusion of the chaparral plain in between two spurs of the Sierra Seri. The deer often feed here and it is easier to see them, as they are confined in a smaller space. Deer tracks were plentiful, many coming across the sand to the water. Francisco led and we walked rapidly up between the spurs and suddenly he pointed. At the same time I saw a doe not seventy-five yards away. She fell at my shot, and as we approached, another doe ran through the chaparral, and then a fawn. I did not have a chance for a shot. The doe was very young but her udder was full of milk and she was the mother of a fawn. We left her and tramped for two hours, covering the whole rinconada, but saw nothing and returned to the doe and skinned her. Then Francisco brought all the meat to the shore, made a smoke, and left it for others to bring in.

We crossed the sierra to hunt the other side. I had only eaten a little oatmeal at daylight, yet I could tramp and climb all day without getting tired. We circled among the ridges and rinconadas but saw nothing and returned to camp long after dark.

Pablo and Rosario (still living with us) were there with two mules and two horses. Three more Seris had come over—all were filling up with meat and most of it was toasting on spits before the fire. There was no water left. A Seri had speared about 15 crabs and we boiled some in sea water, others were buried in the coals of the fire. They were delicious.

The Seris assert that mule deer, rabbits, lions, coyotes, jaguars, and rattlesnakes swim back and forth from the mainland to Tiburón. I have asked all of them and have been very careful that they understood, and they still assert this. They also say sheep never wander out in the chaparral except in the usual places between and near mountains. They are always high up. I have not found sheep tracks here along the bases of the mountains as in the desert ranges farther north. They say the sheep of Cerro Tepopa never leave it – they are therefore isolated there.

Another strange, wild scene about the fire tonight. The canoe was sent back to bring water in the morning. There is a young girl here. She simply lay down in her rags on the far side of her father, away from the fire, and slept on the sand. A cold wind was blowing. I gave her my coat which she seemed glad to get. The other Seris simply slept near the fire, occasionally renewing it during the night. All night long I could see them get up and eat meat. We have no water and I am again thirsty. Near the sea at night everything gets soaked with dew. The Seris pick out splendid places to camp and always sleep in a spot protected from the wind. Everything I have is filled with sand, food and all. I am accustomed to it and grind the sand with my teeth the same as the Seris. I rolled up in the robe.

Dec. 31. This morning, before daylight, all the Seris were sitting around the fire, big pieces of meat roasting on spits. There was nothing left of the meat except a small piece which Pablo saved for me. I roasted it and ate it. I have only a couple of cups of rice and a little tea and sugar left. Pablo brought no food. All are thirsty and we waited a couple of hours for the canoe to come back with water. It came and all drank and I filled my three canteens.

We packed and saddled up. I rode, also Pablo and Rosario, the others walked. Guadalupe and his 12-year-old daughter accompanied us. He is old – a brother of Francisco's. Why they came I know not, except maybe hoping that I would get meat. The little girl, named Moosa, carried a fairly heavy pack on her head, her father nothing. We rode upward about eight miles to a pass called "Yatoom" by the Seris. The mountain on the south, which looks like a splendid one for sheep, the Seris call "Yatoom-mate." Reaching a beautiful spot in the pass, Francisco stopped and said, "Here we make camp." I have felt that if I do not get a buck mule deer from the mainland, my trip would be incomplete, so I decided to spend a day at the pass looking for one—my last chance. Pablo, Rosario, and Romero went on to the wagon, which is 12 miles from here. Burro, Guadalupe, and the girl stayed here. I told them I had no food, that there was scarcely any water, and that they should go on to the wagon, but they stayed, hoping, I know, that I would get meat.

Without eating lunch, Francisco and I started south on the west side of Yatoom-mate, and tramped and tramped over ridges, but saw nothing but whitetail tracks. The mule deer were below in the chaparral. Then we circled and crossed over north of the pass and tramped and tramped, all the time among the foothills. We only saw the tail of a whitetail disappearing in the brush at a distance when almost dark. I found the skull of a peccary.

Reaching camp after dark, I cooked the two cups of rice, made some tea, and divided it among the four. Now we have no food or water. Unless Romero comes back early with food and water, as I had directed him, I cannot hunt. The Indians sit stoically and do not seem to have any thoughts about it. I am really hungry and thirsty and am suffering. Again Moosa curled up like a little animal on the ground on the far side of her father, away from the fire. Again I put my coat over her. It was very picturesque to see the Indians sitting about the fire under a big ironwood tree. I slept close to them. Coyotes, as usual here and on the island, howl in apparent chorus.

Jan. 1, 1922, Sunday. I was up at daylight, the Seris long before, sitting silently about the fire. They always do this before daylight, as it is the coldest hour. As soon as they see any sign of dawn, they sit close to the fire and quietly wait. No food or water! I felt great anxiety that I might not be able to hunt today, and I had determined not to spend another day here. But at nine Romero appeared with tortillas and water. I ate heartily and made some tea. Romero persuaded the three Seris to accompany him back to the wagon.

Francisco and I started at a rapid walk north on the east side of the range. For two and a half hours he kept me going diagonally out in the chaparral. I was somewhat discouraged, knowing that getting a buck there would be mere chance. Finally we reached a place where deer tracks were numerous. Then Francisco said, "Deer lying down—tea." We made tea and at two started again, he testing the wind by throwing up dry dirt and watching the direction of the dust. Then he started to rapidly circle to get nearer the mountain. Soon we saw the leg of a deer which had been killed that morning by a lion, or so Francisco insisted, as he said the tracks near there were those of a lion. Nothing else was left, not even the head—the coyotes had taken it away. Francisco says both lions and *tigres* [jaguars] hunt in the chaparral at night and go to the mountains for the day. Soon he turned against the wind and began to walk slowly, watching, just as I would have done. Back and forth, up and down, we kept on, noiselessly as possible, always looking.

When dung looked fresh, Francisco would kick it, turning it over to note the underside. Often when tracks appeared fresh, he would turn over the adjacent earth with his foot to compare it with the tracks. We noticed fresh tracks but did not follow them. We simply took the chance of having good luck in coming close to a deer, seeing it in time to shoot it. Francisco has the habit of continually watching more to his left and only occasionally swings his head to the right. His eyes are very keen and his great advantage as a hunter is that he can read the ground, knows whether tracks are fresh or old, and knows where the deer are most likely to be found. Otherwise, I feel that I can hunt with more judgment.

I flushed a small owl from some brush and it flew into a hole in a sahueso. I had Francisco cut a long ocotillo branch that was hooked at the end and reached it up and blocked the hole. Then, taking his big knife, I hacked away, deep enough to weaken the sahueso, and pulled it down. We cut out the hole and found the bird uninjured at the bottom. I killed it and put it in my rucksack.

About 3 p.m., as Francisco was looking to the left, I saw the horns of a very large buck passing swiftly through the brush directly ahead, not a hundred feet away. I touched Francisco's shoulder. He saw the horns as they were again disclosed for a moment and rushed forward, a very bad thing to do. I followed but the buck was not seen again. I felt greatly discouraged to miss the chance, but the chaparral was too dense. The buck had heard us and was watching us from behind a tree until he started to run.

We kept on the same way for another hour. Then both of us at the same time saw a young buck standing broadside, about 75 yards to the right in plain sight, looking at us. My offhand shot struck him squarely in the heart. He dropped his head and dashed forward at a gallop into the brush and out of sight. We heard him fall. We approached carefully, hoping another might be there, but none appeared.

There was my buck, with fair horns amply large enough for a comparative specimen, stretched dead before me on a level spot. I took a photograph as he lay, then carefully measured him, and set to work skinning him. He was larger than the deer of Tiburón Island, as was the doe killed on the mainland. He was fairly fat, but the deer here are not nearly so fat as those on the island. Four large wriggling larvae over an inch long fell out of his nose.

The skin was off just before dark. We dressed out the meat and hung it in a sahueso and, taking the skin and horns, started rapidly for camp. It was a long distance away and Francisco fairly trotted, and I had to struggle to keep up. The Seris don't like to travel in the dark, as the cactus hurts their bare feet and legs. But darkness overtook us, and then we went more slowly. It was ten p.m. when we reached camp.

Now I feel the trip is a complete success for I have collected all the available deer and sheep. I have had no time to set traps for small animals. Early this a.m. I collected all the types of cactus I could find and put them in a box. While skinning the deer, my knife pierced my hand, almost transfixing it, and it is very sore. My hunting is ended and my thoughts are of loved ones at home. It has been a wonderful, fascinating trip and unique in

A fine, large ironwood tree, one of the most useful plants in Seriland. Charles Sheldon.

my experience because of the Seris. Late at night it began to rain and everything got soaked. I simply wrapped my robe about me and let it get wet. Francisco got up and crouched by the fire. I am in complete Indian condition and can live as they do.

All day I found myself casting my glasses up toward the mountains to look for sheep. No other animal offers such magnificent sport because it is the most difficult to hunt. Shall I ever hunt them again? Will I again know the joys of the upper world and be intoxicated by the panoramas and views?

Jan. 2, Monday. This morning I prepared the skin and skull, and about noon Rosario and Romero came with a mule and a horse. Last night, while it rained, Francisco and I both lay close to the fire of ironwood. What value the ironwood is to the people of this desert! It provides wonderful fuel and these

Indians, who live without blankets, depend on it, as do the Mexicans. It provides shade and good feed for horses and stock – all
like to browse on its leaves. But its short thorns are sharp and
vicious. The Mexican name for it is *palo fierro*.

We packed the mule and Rosario and Francisco took my
horse and started for the meat. I shouldered my rifle and heavy
rucksack and Romero led the mule and we walked 15 miles
down through the chaparral to Rancho Machoco, an old abandoned building and well near Playa San Bartolo, as all here call
it, different from the name on McGee's map [Playa Noriega].
Here was Pablo with a horse and several Seris, including
Romero's wife and children. Just before dark, Francisco and
Rosario came in with the meat and there was great feasting.
Practically all my food is gone. Everybody has eaten it up and
how we shall eat getting back, I don't know. I gave Santo Blanco
and Burro suits of overalls, which pleased them. Francisco
announced that he, Burro, and Romero are going to Hermosillo
with me. Evidently they expect good rewards, which, of course, I
must give them.

From my own observations, and from talking with the Indians and Mexicans, I have learned a number of things about the
Seris and their way of life. There are two bands of Seris. One of
15 to 18 families lives on Tiburón Island at Armen and ranges
out from there. The other lives at Pozo Coyote on the mainland
and ranges through that country. Juan Tomás is chief of the latter band, Ramón Blanco subchief. Francisco Molina is chief of
the former band, Burro Alazán subchief.

McGee says the Seris never camp near fresh water out of
fear [of attack]. They do camp near water when it is convenient,
but it is seldom convenient for the reason that there is no food
supply near water. They do, however, camp near Pozo Coyote
and go 10 miles to the sea for food. Elsewhere it is easier for
them to camp near food and bring water. This is true at Armen
where fresh water is nine or ten miles away and several people go
every day to bring it.

In summer, the sea provides abundant food. In the winter it
provides little and the Seris travel about and beg at the ranches.
Once in a while they work a little at Costa Rica Ranch, but only

enough to get some clothes. They cannot break away from their wild, free life. For six months they live in hunger, and always have. Then they cannot keep from killing and stealing horses and stock in spite of severe lessons. This is the main reason why they have been so depopulated by the ranchmen. Also, the fishermen from Guaymas have intruded on the Seri fishing grounds with nets and this has led to trouble. The Mexican government does not attempt to do anything for them. They are still fierce and treacherous, but any person with tact and experience with such people can get along with them if he approaches them in the right way. I would not care to have landed on the island a complete stranger to them. I believe that in the past they have been savage and have committed murder and theft during their periods of hunger. They get drunk when cactus fruit, which they know how to ferment, is in season. Like many other Indians, they are said to be crazy to get any alcoholic drink.

The Seris are monogamous and the men seem fond of their wives and children. The mothers are also very fond of their children. The children play as do other Indian children, but they are not obtrusive with a stranger.

Sometimes I observed the Seris assisting each other, at other times not. Burro had cigarettes in camp but gave not one to Francisco who had none. The women continually examine the hair and heads of the men for vermin. They comb the hair with a little brush of twigs tied together like a round whisk broom. The men are fond of having their hair dressed and when they set out to travel they always have it braided. Otherwise they leave it unkempt.

Most of the men have rifles but few cartridges. There are only two or three deer hunters among them and Francisco is the best. They have practically lost the art of shooting the bow. Judging from Francisco's effort to lift deer into trees, I do not think the men are very strong in the arms. But their legs and backs are very powerful.

I observed no illness among them, no eye trouble or catarrhal troubles, coughing, or anything of that kind. All seemed in splendid health. I did not see many aged among them, however. They like blankets if they can get them. They accepted

Pablo Vega drives the wagon on the slow trip to Hermosillo. Charles Sheldon.

all the shelter I could give them. They are very musical.

The Seris have many dogs. There are fifteen or more families at Armen and all had several dogs, curs of all classes. They watch the houses and live in them unrestricted. The dogs are not at all vicious and did not pay any attention to me. They even responded to my petting. But the most surprising thing about them is their discipline. They do not steal meat when the Seris have it—that is, when the Seris are present. Many dogs at a time would push their noses against the meat but, although famished and ravenous, they would not grab it. Probably they have been taught better.

My hunting is ended and now to get back. My stock is weak from lack of food, I have no pack saddles that can be used, and I must depend on wagons as I go along. When will I ever get to Hermosillo?

Jan. 3, Tuesday. Up at daybreak and ready to start, but the stock had wandered off and I did not get started until noon. We could go no farther than La Libertad and here I am to spend the night. I will take the light wagon to Hermosillo, but the heavy wagon must also be brought back to Rancho Palo Alto. That means two mules to each and slow traveling. The ranch people, themselves half-starved, are most hospitable and give me food. I must in some way repay them.

While I have been here the climate has been the most perfect I have ever experienced. The sun is never too hot, there are always breezes, and it is mild and lovely. It is damp near the sea. McGee speaks of the terrible winds blowing continually through Sierra Seri, etc., but I can only say that there have been no winds since I have been here stronger than breezes, except for one night, and only one or two sufficient to raise whitecaps in the strait.

A few Seris are still camped here. The men all have big knives, never carried in sheaths. Because they have no sheaths, they carry them in their back pockets (when they have them), the points sticking up, or pushed through thongs wound around their waists. The knives are in a dangerous position if they fall. They use their knives to chop as with a machete. They are not at all skillful at whittling, but the knife is one of their most useful implements.

The Seri men carry their packs suspended on the ends of a single bar, so placing it over one shoulder as to balance it. While walking they keep shifting it from one shoulder to the other. The best wood for this is palo blanco. The bar is slightly bowed. The women carry packs in baskets placed in holders which fit the head. Both men and women always have an erect carriage in walking like the women of Jamaica. All toe out when they walk. They fairly slide along and it is a fine sight to see them traveling. All are awkward in climbing mountains and they have never climbed or roamed high up among the peaks. They are at home in the level chaparral country and along the coast. They are very quick to see everything along the trail and can read the tracks on the ground and the results of animals' feeding activities. They tell me they can travel two days without water without much discomfort, and going several days without food is common to them. A good fill-up lasts them.

They paddle well but pay no attention to balancing the boat. I saw no native reed boats, *pangas* [*balsas*], but they informed me that the Pozo Coyote band has two. They only have the one boat at Armen. They say they are strong swimmers and often swim across the strait, two or three miles, with their clothes tied to their heads.

The men always have a cloth or gunny sack around their waists wrapped with cow- or deerhide thongs. These thongs they use as the occasion may require for tying up packs and tying loads to the bars. The apron they use to put on the ground or to cover the side away from the fire when sleeping. Their fire is small and all night they keep breaking up the coals and renewing it. It is always of dry ironwood, which is abundant everywhere.

They have a splendid system of smoke signals and can tell when they see smokes just what they mean. Thus they can communicate at a distance all through their land. They know just where to make smoke so that it can be seen and are always looking for smokes.

Their *jacales* are very loosely constructed of the heart-ribs of the sahuaro or ocotillo branches, which are bent over and covered with brush, sea turtle shells, or anything. They hollow out the ground under it and have a fire in the center, nothing else. It does not shed rain—when it rains they sit huddled close to the fire and the women cover the children as best they can. They have almost nothing. Their clothes are rags sewn together or anything they can beg. The same for hats. All are thoroughly infected with lice.

They are jovial and laugh a great deal. When they have food in the pueblo they eat and do nothing else except gamble at cards. They bet cigarettes, cartridges, anything, also small whittled sticks which probably are credits for something. I did not observe them sleeping much in the daytime. The men sang some of the songs for me that they sing to beseech their idols.

Their *ollas* are mostly large, holding five gallons. In them they boil and cook food, and parch corn, when they can get it, by heating sand and shaking the corn in it. They are fond of the fat of animals and also marrow.

Some are very thievish when they have the opportunity, and the fact that Romero and one or two others so carefully

On the road to Hermosillo. Left to right, Chapo, Guadalupe, and Adolpho. Charles Sheldon.

guarded my things on the island shows that some of them cannot be trusted. I saw no immodesty of any kind, no coarseness of talk. The Mexicans use coarse speech when they talk to them. The women at times have sweet voices, but mostly they shriek haglike. Often the girls, when singing, have voices resembling those of our girls. Some of the women are fine-looking when

182

young, and some when older bear traces of pretty faces. Most of
the women hold their heads down in the presence of Mexicans
or when near the ranches, and glance upward or from side to
side. This gives them a furtive look. But on the island I did not
observe these expressions.

They have names for all objective things but I have not been
able to get from them any words showing they understand
abstractions. Their language does not sound nearly so difficult to
pronounce as that of many other Indians I have heard. Their
voices are mostly full and sonorous, but Francisco's is thinner.
He is the ablest among them and can apparently do everything
better than the rest. He is chief by having superior abilities. He
is the most graceful traveler and glides along without effort. I
could observe no organization in their life, but they seem to
obey the chief, who does not, however, make any demands that
are distasteful to them.

Tonight I set some traps for kangaroo rats. I passed the evening chatting at the ranch, then prepared my blankets for bed.

Jan. 4, Wednesday. I caught two rats and skinned them. Then
we loaded the two wagons, two mules to each, and started and
came to Palo Alto Ranch. Francisco, Romero, Burro, and
Guadalupe, and two other Seris, Chapo and Adolpho, came
along, walking, all bound for Hermosillo. The Seris were given
meat here. They are traveling without food or blankets or anything. They trust to the ranchmen to give them a little to eat or
they go without. I am now on the home stretch, but the stock is
in poor condition.

The Seris say the jaguar eats out the throat and heart of his
kills and takes little more. The cougar eats it all. This is why
Francisco said it was a cougar that killed the deer, a leg of which
we saw in the chaparral.

Almost nobody ever hunts sheep here. The Seris never
hunted them until they got rifles and then only when they hap-
pened to see one low on the smaller ranges. Food is so abundant
that it seems these mountains could support a large number of
sheep, but, as elsewhere in the desert ranges, sheep are not as
abundant as in the Rockies of the far north. Perhaps severe

droughts wipe out a great many and keep down the increase. All have large numbers of ticks in their ears—perhaps the ticks cause many of them to die in summer or when the drought conditions are bad. Their habits are the same as desert sheep elsewhere. They live on the high crags.

The Papago Indians hunt the mule deer in the chaparral, mostly for their hides. If the country settles more they will exterminate them. Mule deer are more abundant on the coast side of Sierra Seri where they are not so much hunted. They are wild and difficult to hunt. Peccary trails are seen everywhere, but they mostly stay in the thick jungle in the daytime. Whitetail deer are higher on the slopes and only occasionally below in the chaparral. They rut in January. They are very wild but abundant.

The Seris do not seem to try to conceal anything about topographical features of their country, but answer all questions in regard to water or anything. I have not had the chance to observe their fishing, which is, of course, one of the principal features of their life. They have no modern fishing equipment or other implements except knives. They seem willing and anxious for civilized clothes and comforts but will not work to get them. Nothing can destroy their life of freedom.

The Seris know many of the stars and constellations and have names for them. They know north by the north star. They say that all other stars walk around the heavens but the north star remains where it is. They know the planets. They say they have no calendar and do not recognize a new year. They reckon time by the sun, moon, Pleiades, and other constellations. They reckon tides by the sun and moon.

Young children under eight run along with the adults, but if tired the men carry them. The women on the march carry their infants. They don't travel at night if they can avoid it and don't see in the dark better than other people. The unmarried girls do not drink, but married women do. It is said that when intoxicated the men often cut each other up with knives. They never mingle sexually with the Mexicans because they are afraid of venereal diseases. Mexicans inform me that the Seris are often coarse, but I did not see it at Armen and am inclined to think that since the Mexicans always talk coarsely to them, the Seris

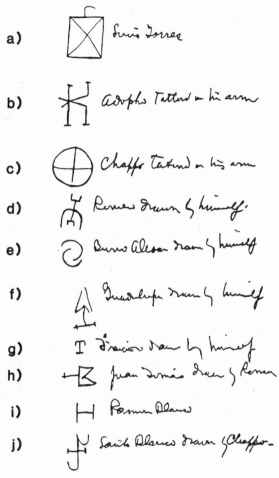

Seri "signatures" drawn in Charles Sheldon's journal: a. Luis Torres; b. Adolpho, tattooed on his arm; c. Chapo, tattooed on his arm; d. Romero, drawn by himself; e. Burro Alazán, drawn by himself; f. Guadalupe, drawn by himself; g. Francisco, drawn by himself; h. Juan Tomás, drawn by Ramón; i. Ramón Blanco, drawn by himself; j. Santo Blanco, drawn by Chapo.

respond in kind, thinking that is what the Mexicans want. They only come in contact with the lower class of Mexicans.

Most of the men have their signatures tattooed in faint black lines on their left forearms. Late this p.m. I had some of

the Seris write their signatures for me in this journal. The night
is cold and they have four small fires.

Jan. 5, Thursday. This morning we were up early but there was
the usual delay in getting breakfast and we did not get started
until 10 a.m. We reached Costa Rica Ranch late in the p.m., the
Seris having preceded us. We left the big wagon at Palo Alto and
have four mules on the small wagon. In one place on the incom-
ing trip I saw fourteen or fifteen caracaras, and in the same place
I noticed them again. This was north of Palo Alto. J. L. Blevins
put us up and gave us food. I paid Antonio Castillo, the Papago,
a fine old fellow but too old to do much.

The Seri women make their baskets from a species of torote,
Jatropha spathulata, called *matacora* by the Mexicans. They tear
it into strips with their teeth. The main ribs of the baskets are
composed of several of these strands, and around these they
wind and fasten other strips which they push through with a
bone awl.

In their village I found very few things either for fishing or
any other means of making a living, scarcely any tools, not
much pottery—a few ollas, mostly large, but one small one. Not
one Indian had a blanket or anything to cover him while sleeping. They have almost nothing and one finds it difficult to
understand how they can live.

I saw no very old people among them, not one who showed
signs of great age. One man was blind and was taken care of by a
woman. He is the medicine man. I noticed one broad-shouldered
young Indian man about 30 years old with a wife who might
have been sixty.

They say that the former Tepoca Indians, now extinct, were
terrible fighters and the Seris have always been afraid of them.
They have always feared the Papagos. They walk no better than
any other desert Indians who do not belong to sedentary tribes.
The women walk much slower than the men and Romero said
that when women were along they had to go slowly.

Many of the men and women wear brass or tin rings and
also earrings. Some woman have bracelets of tin. The women
and many of the men paint their faces, and many children were

186

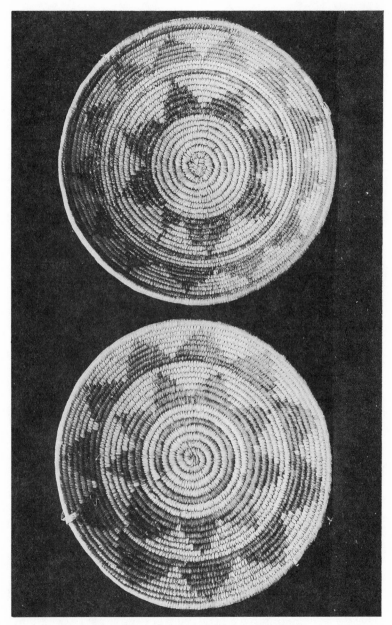

Seri baskets obtained by Charles Sheldon. William G. Sheldon.

painted. Molina was not painted but his wife was constantly painted. The colors are white, blue, and red. They wear cowhide guaraches, though some go barefoot if they don't have them.

The men carry most of the water from long distances. They hunt pelicans at night with torches of pitahaya and clubs, killing the roosting birds. Their turtle spear is 9 paces long and has a two-inch iron spike countersunk in the end. They have very few artifacts.

These Indians are rapid trailers and travelers in the lower country, but they don't like the mountains and never climb the rough, higher ones. They have explored well up the canyons for water, however. The Mexicans can run faster for short distances. The Tarahumaras may be superior to them as long-distance travelers.

A few Seri men are short and sturdy, Santo Blanco for example, also Chapo. Also a few of the men are slender and wiry. But most are tall and well proportioned. Most of the men have no beards, yet Burro and one or two others had scattered hairs growing out which they kept cut with knives. They have scarcely any hair on their bodies. Burro has two bullet marks, one on his right shin, the other at the base of his big toe, made, he said, by "vaqueros." Burro and Francisco told me that they had often been to Angel de la Guarda Island. The Seri men, when not hunting or at the ranches, most of the time do absolutely nothing but simply stand or sit around, at times chatting. They are well aware that strangers fear to come on the island, for three of the men at different times asked me if I was not afraid of them.

I saw no evidence of bad treatment of their wives, in fact they seemed to act most gently toward them. They seemed fond of their children. Some of the women are good looking, even when older. Others look fierce, treacherous, and wily. Some of the girls are pretty. I saw no inclination of quarreling among them, nor do the children quarrel. They laugh a great deal and when together are quite merry and keep up a constant stream of talk. The chiefs evidently have little control over those below them.

They are very fond of sugar and sweets and seem to like any food. They do not eat the meat of coyotes, hawks, owls, loons, or snakes, but are very fond of pelicans and herons. They eat a small cuttlefish. They like salt and pepper if they can get it. Meat and fish are their staples. If they have plenty of other food, they still crave meat. They like horse and burro meat better than that of cattle. They particularly like fat. Francisco was very careful to take all the fat of the deer. They have horse hoofs (I saw two) hanging in their jacales, probably for boiling. They like marrow, and with a rock crack open all possible bones to get it. From all I could learn, they have never been cannibals.

They have learned from the Mexicans how to tan buckskin with brains, but their work is very crude. They seem to make no use whatever of the buckskin, or at least use it very little. They bring the skins to the ranches to trade. They use sinew for sewing. The men sew better than the women.

They know almost nothing about money, cannot count it, yet they have a vague idea that it has purchasing power and they will take it. One can buy or trade for their baskets for almost nothing. Romero gave a woman five lumps of sugar for a fine basket, and two lumps for a necklace.

I had no opportunity to learn about the Seris' clans, totems, marriage ceremony, the symbolism of their face painting, etc. Much of what McGee has written about the Seris is inconsistent with what I saw. As he only saw them for a week at Rancho Costa Rica, how could he have penetrated the facts? I fear that much of what he wrote exists only in his imagination.

I slept on a stretched canvas last night, which was not comfortable. We got some eggs and honey, which were luxuries.

Jan. 6, Friday. We had a late breakfast and made a late start, but after the first six miles the road was good and the mules trotted. We kept going long after dark, having (I thought) left the Seris far behind. Burro held the reins, Pablo rode on a horse on one side, beating the mules, I rode on the other. We made about 30 miles without stopping except for a moment at a ranch to water the stock. Before we got the mules unhitched the Seris appeared.

There is scarcely any wood here and we have not an atom of food—only some water. The Seris had not eaten any breakfast. I am hungry, but they sit by the fire and are cheerful. They tell me when they have run hard for a whole day and are very tired, they, by means of a knife, draw a quantity of blood from the calves of their legs and this relieves them. They slept almost without any fire, no blankets, and there is frost tonight and the air is cold. It is much colder away from the sea. The stock is very low from want of food and I have to steel my nerves to endure pushing the poor animals ahead. Coyotes howl and yell as they have every night on the whole trip, including on the island.

Jan. 7, Saturday. We were up at daylight, hitched the mules, saddled, and hastened forward, all very hungry. It was a strange sight to see the mules trotting, Pablo, the vaquero, riding along one side yelling and beating them, I on the other side to keep them in the road, Burro, the Seri, sitting motionless holding the reins, while the five other Seris kept along at a trot. Later, Mexicans in strange costumes passed us and all stopped to see the wild Indians.

When within six miles of Hermosillo, I galloped my poor horse ahead and at 2:30 reached the telegraph office and sent a telegram to Louisa. Then I went to get her letters and read them all. Then came a royal bath and civilized clothes. The wagon came bearing my trophies and I went out to arrange to have them packed so that I will not be delayed in getting away from here. The Seris are to come here in the morning. Great crowds gathered to see my heads. Now my only thought is to hasten home. Even after two hard days of riding, I did not eat anything until 7 p.m., the first mouthful since yesterday morning. Now I can endure hunger and irregular eating. I feel that I could, after a long period of similar living, adapt to the food deprivation of the Seris.

Jan. 8. Sunday and I can do nothing. The Seris came into town and I gave all a dinner in the back of the hotel. Crowds came in to see them. Crowds follow them through the streets. The Seris seem very wild. They cross the street single file, and when they see a motor approaching they all run, at the same time holding up their hands, not believing it can stop.

I arranged to have my material packed, and endured the day—a day of strange sensations in a Mexican town. No people on the street, no life or gaiety, all is like a graveyard. The people have nothing and are hungry. Their ambition is gone, the result of revolution and bad government.

Jan. 9, Monday. At daylight the Seris were at the hotel. Soon I took them out to a store, crowds surrounding us. I gave them much cloth, blankets, needles, thread, tobacco, dye for painting their faces, hats, overalls, knives, fishing tackle, matches, and much other stuff. They preferred common butcher knives to machetes, which I offered them.

I have eighteen of their baskets, many necklaces, their strange violin, ancient stones used as pendants, and Francisco's chief's stone, the best prize, on which is a crude painting suggesting Armen with lines indicating trails leading to it.

Then I said good-bye, hastened to get my material off by express, and caught the 11 a.m. train and reached Nogales at 8:30 p.m., where I spent the night.

Jan. 10. After getting things through the customs house, I motored for 2½ hours to Tucson and boarded the Sunset Limited train late at night. My trip has ended.

Desert bighorn sheep. Courtesy Bob Miles, Arizona Game and Fish Department, Phoenix.

Epilogue

CHARLES SHELDON'S SOUTHWEST LEGACY

Were he to return to his Southwest hunting grounds, Charles Sheldon would be both pleased and surprised. He would be delighted to learn that most of the areas he hunted in Arizona and Sonora remain relatively wild and inhabited by mountain sheep. He would probably be amazed to learn that bighorn sheep, as we now call them, are legally hunted in some of the places he sought them more than seventy years ago. He would be especially gratified to learn that several of his sheep-hunting locales are now within national parks, national wildlife refuges, and designated wilderness areas. How this all came to be is in itself an interesting story and one that Sheldon helped pioneer in several ways.

When Sheldon undertook his mission to collect a series of mountain sheep from the Southwest deserts for the National Museum, the sheep of the region were in serious trouble. So severe and rapid had been the decline in desert sheep numbers that most U.S. states and territories having the animal had en-acted legislation giving it complete protection. The Arizona ter-ritorial legislature, for example, had passed a five-year morato-rium against the taking of mountain sheep in 1893. In 1897, mountain sheep were permanently protected—a status that was continued in the new state game code of 1913. So pessimistic was the prognosis for the animal's survival that Edgar Mearns in his 1907 work on Arizona mammals stated, "The opinion is general among the white settlers along the Mexican border in that region that the bighorn sheep is doomed to extinction at an early period." Most other conservationists of the day had come to the same conclusion, including William T. Hornaday, who had hunted sheep in some of the same country in Sonora as Sheldon.

Desert bighorn sheep populations continued to decline through the early 1900s with or without legal protection. The conventional wisdom for the increasing scarcity of sheep was unregulated hunting by Indians with modern firearms and the shooting of sheep by prospectors, miners, and settlers for "camp meat." Hence, the demand for closed seasons continued, even though the enforcement of such edicts was difficult and largely ineffectual. In truth, the causes for the decline in Southwest sheep numbers were far too complex and enigmatic to be understood by even the most astute naturalists of the day. Only after years of study has it been shown, with almost absolute certainty, that catastrophic declines in bighorn sheep numbers are the result of exposure to livestock-borne diseases and competition for scarce forage and water brought on by the introduction of domestic sheep, goats, cattle, and burros to the bighorn's range. Sheldon noted the presence of some wild horses in the Grand Canyon in 1912 and observed more than one hundred wild burros from one vantage point in the Sierra Pinacate in 1915. He also reported seeing the tracks of cattle far out in the desert south of Wellton, Arizona, during the wet winter of 1914–1915. Clearly, some livestock, at least, were already encroaching on even the most remote desert bighorn ranges at this early date.

With both domestic and feral livestock increasing in distribution and abundance throughout the Southwest, bighorn herds continued to languish through the 1920s. Ironically, the reduction in sheep range and numbers in the more arid reaches of western Arizona and Sonora was less severe than elsewhere, but only because there were fewer livestock in the desert. Nonetheless, desert sheep were rightfully judged to be in jeopardy throughout their range, and to preserve his country's big game, Mexican President Álvaro Obregón issued a decree in 1922 totally protecting mountain sheep (*borregos*) and pronghorn antelope (*berrendos*) for ten years. So fearful was W. T. Hornaday that poaching was decimating sheep numbers in Sonora that he persuaded the Mexican government to appoint a special warden to enforce the new decree. This warden, a twenty-year-old American named Ben Tinker, assumed the duty of patrolling the Sonora border country in 1923 and was paid by

W. T. Hornaday's Permanent Wildlife Protection Fund. However, Sonoran officials began issuing "special" sheep-hunting permits to American sportsmen having sufficient money or connections. After complaining without effect to federal officials in Mexico about this practice, Hornaday withdrew his support for the project—leaving Tinker to embark on a career of guiding American sheep hunters. But while such permits continued to be issued for many years, the harvest of an occasional trophy ram or two had little effect on Sonoran sheep numbers.

By 1930, because of the incompatibility of wild sheep with the proliferating herds of domestic sheep, goats, and other livestock, thrifty populations of desert bighorn persisted only in the Grand Canyon and in the most rugged desert mountains. Sportsmen had become convinced that federal wildlife refuges or additional national parks were essential to save their most esteemed game animal—the strategy successfully used by Sheldon for preserving Denali's wildlife. Working with government personnel, several sportsmen-conservationists devised a plan for a federal desert bighorn sheep refuge in southwest Arizona totaling 4,000,000 acres. The major emphasis of the refuge would be the protection of sheep from poachers and predators, although it was assumed that other animals such as desert antelope would also benefit.

The proposal met with a storm of protest. Cattlemen, sheepmen, miners, and local politicians strongly objected to the federal government withdrawing so much real estate from the public domain for what Arizona Governor W. P. Hunt termed "a damned billy goat pasture." To further obfuscate matters, the U.S. Department of the Interior's park and grazing services got into a squabble with the U.S. Biological Survey in the Department of Agriculture over which agency should manage such a refuge. Refuge advocates, who wanted jurisdiction to go to the Biological Survey, were stymied by that bureau then having no legal authority or personnel to manage a big-game refuge. The Park Service, on the other hand, had no prerogative to manage an area primarily for one species of wildlife.

An impasse was avoided through the intercession of Major Frederick R. Burnham, an old Arizona frontiersman and veteran scout of the Boer War, who used his influence as one of the founders of the Boy Scouts of America to enlist the scouts in a crusade for a "desert game range." With Arizona's three Boy Scout councils counteracting opposition from the Arizona Cattle Growers, Arizona Small Mine Operators' Association, and state politicians, game range proponents were able to generate sufficient political support for a sheep refuge. To appease his wrangling bureaucrats, President Franklin D. Roosevelt made a Solomon-like decision. In 1937 he created by executive order a 330,000-acre Organ Pipe Cactus National Monument on the Arizona-Sonora border to be managed by the National Park Service. The following year he withdrew another 1,500,000 acres for the Kofa and Cabeza Prieta national game ranges. These areas would be jointly managed by Interior's Grazing Service and Agriculture's Biological Survey, soon to become, respectively, the Bureau of Land Management and Fish and Wildlife Service within the Department of Interior. Most of the remaining 2,000,000 acres in the original refuge proposal was destined to be withdrawn as gunnery ranges with the onset of World War II. Other real and de facto desert bighorn sanctuaries were created, including Lake Mead National Recreation Area in Arizona and Nevada, the Desert Game Range in Nevada, San Andreas National Wildlife Refuge in New Mexico, Death Valley National Monument in California and Nevada, and Joshua Tree National Monument and Anza-Borrego Desert State Park in California.

Nonetheless, the war years were hard ones for the desert bighorn. The federal game refuges, national monuments, and other desert sheep ranges continued to be leased to cattlemen, and because of the high demand for beef, stocking rates were often excessive. Feral burros proliferated. Interest in desert bighorns diminished. A. A. Nichol, a biologist who conducted a sheep survey in Arizona for the Audubon Society in the late 1930s, thought, like his earlier colleagues, that the desert bighorn was destined to survive only in token numbers if not doomed to disappear entirely.

A major turning point in the battle to save the desert bighorn was Arizona Game and Fish Department biologist John

Russo's study of desert bighorn sheep, which began in 1950. This ambitious five-year investigation in western Arizona sought to learn the bighorn's food, water, and habitat requirements and determine what factors were preventing the animals from increasing. To accomplish these objectives, Russo developed new survey techniques and devised a method for estimating population sizes. For the project to succeed, it was also necessary to delineate the bighorn's present and past distribution throughout the state, compile a list of beneficial management practices, evaluate the effects of limited hunting for trophy rams, and investigate the feasibility of restocking desert bighorn sheep into suitable historical ranges.

After an outbreak of sheep lung disease in 1952, Russo realized that the transmission of ungulate pathogens was the major obstacle to the bighorn's recovery. He emphasized the need to separate bighorn sheep from livestock and feral burros, and recommended the removal of domestic animals from bighorn habitat. He also instituted a tightly controlled sheep-hunting program that allowed the taking of trophy rams, and initiated a bighorn sheep trapping and transplanting project—programs that were eventually adopted by other southwestern states including Sonora and Baja California.

Legal trophy hunting served to intensify interest in bighorn sheep management among sportsmen and brought needed public attention to the animal's requirements. Without public hunting and an ongoing management program, there would have been little demand for transplants and less concern about sheep/livestock conflicts. Shortly after Russo's study and the legalization of public hunting in the 1950s, several organizations were formed to champion sheep causes, beginning with the Desert Bighorn Council (consisting primarily of professional sheep biologists). Sheep hunters followed suit, forming the Fraternity of Desert Bighorn Sheep in Nevada, the Arizona Desert Bighorn Sheep Society, the Foundation for North American Wild Sheep, and, most recently, the California Sheep Society. Not only did these groups provide a political voice for desert sheep, they would eventually raise hundreds of thousands of dollars each year to fund transplants, develop water holes, and initiate other programs designed to increase sheep numbers and protect sheep habitat.

With professional management and public support, the status of desert bighorn greatly improved. By the early 1980s all livestock, owned and feral, had been removed from Organ Pipe Cactus National Monument and the Kofa and Cabeza Prieta game refuges. Wild burros were eliminated or greatly reduced on Park Service lands in the Grand Canyon and on parts of Lake Mead National Recreation Area, and from several mountain ranges managed by the Bureau of Land Management. Domestic sheep were recognized as being incompatible with wild sheep, and domestic sheep-grazing leases have been terminated on all federal lands having desert bighorn populations. In 1990, the United States Congress proclaimed that more than 90 percent of the Kofa and Cabeza Prieta game refuges, and hundreds of thousands of acres of BLM lands in Arizona, be managed as wilderness. This legislation precluded further construction of roads, communication towers, and other facilities that have encroached on lambing grounds and other key bighorn habitats. Most of Grand Canyon National Park, Organ Pipe "Cactus" National Monument, and Lake Mead National Recreation Area have also been set aside as wilderness or recommended for wilderness status.

With livestock-free refuges providing a supply of desert bighorn for transplanting to vacant habitats, large-scale reintroduction programs became biologically feasible. Furthermore, the development of new capture techniques involving the use of supercharged helicopters, sophisticated sedative drugs delivered by special guns, and effective net guns made such programs economically efficient. The result is that the desert bighorn is now making a substantial comeback. Annual surpluses of wild sheep in the Kofa National Wildlife Refuge and the Plomosa Mountains in western Arizona, Lake Mead National Recreation Area, and other localities have enabled biologists to return bighorn sheep to dozens of Southwestern mountain ranges from which they had been extirpated. These transplants, coupled with other conservation measures, have resulted in population estimates for desert sheep increasing from 14,800 in 1978 to

23,500 in 1989. These estimates would have been even higher if it had not been for the continued decline of mountain sheep in New Mexico, Texas, Chihuahua, and Coahuila, where diseases borne by domestic sheep, goats, and other livestock continue to thwart restoration attempts.

Despite past competition with feral burros and bouts with exotic diseases, bighorn sheep persist in the lower reaches of the Grand Canyon, where they are commonly seen by hikers and river runners. And their future in the canyon appears promising. In 1979, Grand Canyon National Park was expanded to include most of Grand Canyon National Monument and large areas of the Kaibab National Forest. Ninety-three percent of the park, including the area hunted by Sheldon, is now managed by the Park Service as wilderness. That more of Sheldon's Grand Canyon hunting grounds is not wilderness is due to Congress increasing the size of the Havasupai Indian Reservation from a mere 500 acres to 160,000 acres in 1975.

Bighorn sheep are still present and legally hunted in Sheldon's old hunting grounds in the Gila, Tinajas Altas, Cabeza Prieta, and Tule Mountains in Arizona. The Cabeza Prieta and Tule mountains are now within the Cabeza Prieta National Wildlife Refuge. The southern portion of the Gila Mountains and the entire Tinajas Altas range are included within the 2,660,000-acre Barry M. Goldwater Gunnery Range, which is closed to livestock grazing.

In 1979 the Sierra Pinacate was designated by the Mexican government as the Pinacate Protected Forestry Zone, a kind of national park. A bi-national group, "Amigos del Pinacate," assists in funding various administrative and field projects within the zone, installs "protected zone" notices, and picks up trash. Although cattle grazing occurs in and around the Sierra Pinacate, and a cinder mine is located within the protected zone, this unique area remains relatively intact. Bighorn populations in the Pinacate are low compared to those in some other desert ranges, but sheep appear to be on the increase. Both bighorn sheep and Sonoran pronghorn, and their sign, are now frequently observed on and near the mountain. In the 1950s, bighorn were reported to have been extirpated in the Sierra Pinacate, but fortunately these reports were in error.

The small, isolated Sierra del Rosario is an exception to the current improving status of desert sheep in Sheldon's old hunting haunts. It appears that bighorn sheep are no longer present in this arid and waterless range where Sheldon bagged a ram and found a ewe's skull in 1916. At least no droppings, beds, or other sign of sheep could be found on a hike to one of the range's summits on a short visit to these mountains in January 1992. What we did find was an abundance of goat droppings in the vicinity of an abandoned herder's cave formed by two enormous boulders at the western base of the mountains. Numerous live goats were also seen in the Sierra Viejo a few miles to the northeast. The Sierra del Rosario, like so many Sonoran mountains, has also been visited by woodcutters in their incessant quest for firewood.

At the time of Sheldon's visit, the Seri Indians numbered no more than 200 individuals. They were a small remnant of a once much more numerous people—there may have been 3,000 Seris at the time of their first contact with Europeans in the 1600s. But wars with the Spanish and then the Mexicans subtracted from their population, and European diseases took a heavy toll. That their culture survived at all was due to the extreme aridity of their homeland. The Seri country was unsuited to farming or stock raising, and outsiders found little of value there. The Seris themselves remained fishermen and sea turtle hunters isolated from the Mexican mainstream.

The fear and suspicion that had characterized Seri-Mexican relations for centuries began to soften in the late 1920s. In the 1930s the Indians began fishing commercially on a small scale, selling their catch of fish and sea turtles to Mexican buyers. After World War II, outboard motors were introduced, but the Seris continued to make their own wooden boats and their fishing methods remained simple. Sea turtles, once a staple in the Seri diet, became increasingly scarce in the region during the second half of the twentieth century owing to heavy exploitation by both Seris and Mexicans.

In the 1960s a market developed in the United States for Seri handicrafts, especially ironwood carvings, a new, nontraditional product. Almost overnight, the sale to traders and tourists of beautifully carved animal figures, along with traditional items such as baskets and seashell necklaces, became an important source of cash for the Seris. This commerce and improved roads brought outsiders into the Seri country in increasing numbers.

Today, pickup trucks are seen in Seriland, and small concrete-block houses have replaced their old brush shelters in the Seri villages on the mainland coast. Fiberglass boats have supplanted the homemade wooden ones. The Seri population has grown to about 1,000 people and literacy is on the rise—the acculturation process continues. Life is easier now than when Charles Sheldon visited the Seris, but the summer sun blazes just as fiercely, and fishing in the stormy gulf, always a dangerous business in small craft, remains a tribal mainstay. The Seris have retained their language, their sense of humor, and many unique aspects of their fascinating culture. They are still people of the desert and sea.

Less satisfactory to the Seris has been the history of their tenure on Tiburón Island. In the 1960s, the Mexican government declared the islands of the Gulf of California to be marine nature reserves and Tiburón a federal wildlife refuge. All of the Seris were removed to encampments on the mainland, and the island was declared off limits to all but those holding special visitor's permits. These restrictions have since been relaxed, but the island remains uninhabited. In 1975, 20 desert bighorn were captured in the Sierra Seri by Mexican and American biologists and transplanted by helicopter to Sierra Kunkaak on Tiburón Island. A survey by Mexican biologists in December 1987, and a visit to the summit of Sierra Kunkaak by the editors during the spring of 1991, indicate that the transplanted sheep have spread out and occupied the island's rugged sierras. A recent helicopter survey resulted in a population estimate, which is almost certainly conservative, of between 50 and 100 sheep for livestock-free Tiburón Island. Thankfully, shed antlers and droppings show that Tiburón's *bura* are still present in reasonable numbers despite the introduction of a competing hoofed animal.

The Mexican government is said to recognize the Seri Indians' claim to their ancestoral homeland in the Sierra Seri. The Indians, besides hunting there themselves, are given regulatory control over the taking of deer and other game in these mountains by Mexicans and Americans—or so we are told. Whatever the mountain's legal status, bighorn sheep, mule deer, white-tailed deer, and javelina are all still present in the Sierra Seri.

Alas, the scientists in Washington never did devise a satisfactory taxonomic classification for mountain sheep. By 1937, C. H. Merriam and his colleagues had proposed no fewer than four species and two subspecies of bighorn sheep as inhabiting the deserts of the southwestern United States and northwestern Mexico. Basing their classifications on skull measurements, pelage characters, and imperfectly known distributions, Merriam and his disciples were notorious for "creating" new species and subspecies. For example, Merriam proposed four different species of grizzly bear for Arizona alone. Confusion thus reigned over the taxonomic status of bighorn sheep in the United States for years. In 1940, in an attempt at a more realistic classification, Ian McTaggart Cowan, using a larger series of skull measurements and better distributional information, classified all desert bighorn as being only races of *Ovis canadensis*, the Rocky Mountain bighorn—a conclusion reached by British sheep expert Richard Lydekker in 1913.

Cowan recognized four subspecies of desert bighorns. He considered the Nelson bighorn (*Ovis canadensis nelsoni*) to be an essentially Mojave desert form, and retained the two races of bighorns in extreme southern California and Baja California (the peninsular bighorn, *O. c. cremnobates*, and Weems bighorn, *O. c. weemsi*). He lumped all the remaining mainland desert bighorns in the subspecies *O. c. mexicana*, the Mexican bighorn, even though he admitted possibly being in error by not recognizing *O. c. gallardi* (Mearns) as a Sonoran Desert race. Acknowledging that these decisions were somewhat subjective, Cowan noted that "Along the valley of the Colorado River the . . . pale desert sheep of Arizona gradually give way to the . . . dark colored sheep inhabiting the Rocky Mountains. The trend is so gradual that it is impossible to draw an arbitrary line between the two." Although Cowan's classification remains essentially unchanged in scientific nomenclature, most sportsmen and biologists use the general term "desert bighorn" for all bighorn sheep inhabiting the Southwest's deserts. In this respect, it should be mentioned that the only desert sheep that Charles Sheldon considered to be significantly different from the others he collected was the unusually small ram he bagged in the isolated Sierra del Rosario. He reported no important differences in the sheep from the Grand Canyon, Tinajas Altas Mountains, Sierra Pinacate, or Sierra Seri.

It can truly be said that Charles Sheldon was the epitome of the wilderness hunter. Today's sheep hunters would be well served to read Sheldon's sheep-hunting accounts and emulate his "go light" ethic. Nothing in the now extensive body of sheep-hunting literature stands the test of time better than Sheldon's descriptions of sheep behavior and sheep hunting. He was among the first to notice that desert sheep girdled saguaros and could obtain the moisture for their existence from dew and desert vegetation. These and other of his astute observations are as valid now as then. His vivid descriptions of climbing to the highest ridges and peaks, his use of field glasses, and his careful stalks are the hallmarks of all successful sheep hunters past and present. But rarely is a modern telling so realistic. Only Jack O' Connor, who also hunted sheep in the arid ranges of Sonora, came close to matching Sheldon's wonderfully descriptive narratives of wilderness sheep hunting. The joy of desert solitude, the evening musings around a campfire, the need to silently place one's foot in just the right place when making a stalk with hands clutched to vertical walls, the frustration of an opportunity lost – no one relates the trials and triumphs of a quest for desert sheep better than Charles Sheldon.

And Sheldon's wildlife and botanical observations are not only of interest to desert sheep hunters. His sightings of Clark's nutcrackers on the south rim of the Grand Canyon, his accurate commentary on the scarcity of mountain lions in extreme western Arizona and Sonora, his notes on the occurrence of white-sided (antelope) jackrabbits and abundant black-tailed jackrabbits, his report of sandhill cranes flying over the Pinacate lava flow, and other observations dutifully recorded in his journal are important benchmarks of earlier animal distributions in pristine desert environments. Nor is his record of the plants and animals he encountered the only information of interest. His reports of rock-walled hunting blinds built by prehistoric Americans in the Grand Canyon and of early rock structures in the Sierra Pinacate are worthy of contemplation by those interested in archaeology. His descriptions of a tinaja-filling deluge and a winter freeze in the Sierra Pinacate provide information useful to geomorphologists and climatologists. His finding fossils in the Sierra del Rosario may one day pique the curiosity of a paleontologist. But most importantly, his lengthy and unbiased account of traditional Seri life is an invaluable contribution to the ethnological record.

It has been said of John C. Frémont that he was the West's foremost pathfinder and that great cities sprang from his camp-fires. If so, it can also be said that Charles Sheldon was one of our most remarkable explorers, and that what arose from his campsites were national parks, wildlife refuges, and wilderness areas. There is no question in our minds which legacy Charles Sheldon would have found the more becoming.

Bibliography

Albright, H. M. 1985. *The Birth of the National Park Service: The Founding Years, 1913–33*. Salt Lake City and Chicago: Howe Bros.

Amundson, G. A. 1942. "The Bighorn Sheep." *Arizona Wildlife and Sportsman* April:1–2.

Annerino, J. 1991. *Adventuring in Arizona*. San Francisco: Sierra Club Books.

Bailey, V. 1912. "A New Subspecies of Mountain Sheep from Western Texas and Southeastern New Mexico." *Proc. Biol. Soc. Washington* 25:109–10.

———. 1935. "Mammals of the Grand Canyon." *Nat. Hist. Assoc. Nat. Hist. Bull.* 1:1–42.

Barclay, G. E. 1947. "Mountain Sheep are Coming Back." *Arizona Wildlife Sportsman* October:10, 11, 22, 23.

Benson, L. 1969. *The Cacti of Arizona*. 3rd ed. Tucson: University of Arizona Press.

Benson, L., and R. A. Darrow. 1981. *Trees and Shrubs of the Southwestern Deserts*. 3rd ed. Tucson: University of Arizona Press.

Bolton, H. E., ed. 1948. *Kino's Historical Memoir of Primeria Alta*. Two vols. in one. Berkeley: University of California Press.

Brown, B. T., S. W. Carothers, and R. R. Johnson. 1987. *Grand Canyon Birds*. Tucson: University of Arizona Press.

Brown, D. E., ed. 1982. "Biotic Communities of the American Southwest—United States and Mexico." *Desert Plants* 4(1–4):1–342.

Brown, D. E. 1984. "Thoughts on Killing a Desert Bighorn." *Safari Magazine* 10(2): 16–19, 53, 59.

———. 1989. "Wilderness, Desert Bighorn, and the American Hunter." *Game Country* 2(1): 46–50.

———. 1990. "A Mexican Sheep Hunt for the 1980's." *Game Country* 2(2): 84–88.

———. 1991. "Land Lost in Time." *Arizona Republic* 8/9:E-4.

Brown, W. E. 1991. *A History of the Denali-Mount McKinley Region, Alaska.* Santa Fe: National Park Service, Southwest Regional Office.

Broyles, B. 1987. "Adventure in the Pinacate." *J. Arizona Hist.* 28(2): 155–88.

Broyles, B., ed. 1988. "W J McGee's 'Desert Thirst as Disease.' " *J. of the Southwest,* 30(2):222–53.

Buechner, H. K. 1960. "The Bighorn Sheep in the United States: Its Past, Present, and Future." *The Wildl. Soc. Wildl. Monog.* 4:1–174.

Burt, W. H. 1938. "Faunal Relationships and Geographic Distribution of Mammals in Sonora, Mexico." Ann Arbor: University of Michigan Misc. Publ. Mus. Zool. No. 39:1–77.

Carmony, N. B., and D. E. Brown, eds. 1983. *Tales from Tiburon.* Phoenix: Southwest Nat. Hist. Assoc.

———. 1991. *Mexican Game Trails.* Norman: University of Oklahoma Press.

Clark, J. L. 1964. *The Great Arc of the Wild Sheep.* Norman: University of Oklahoma Press.

Cook, F. A. 1907. "The Conquest of Mount McKinley." *Harper's Monthly Magazine.* May:821–37.

———. 1908. *To the Top of the Continent.* New York: Doubleday, Page and Co.

Cowan, I. M. 1940. "Distribution and Variation in the Native Sheep of North America." *Amer. Midl. Nat.* 24:505–80.

Desert Bighorn Council 1957–1990. Trans. Desert Bighorn Council (issued annually).

Felger, R. S. 1980. "Vegetation and Flora of the Gran Desierto, Sonora, Mexico." *Desert Plants* 2(2): 87–114.

Felger, R. S., and M. B. Moser. 1985. *People of the Desert and Sea: Ethnobotany of the Seri Indians.* Tucson: University of Arizona Press.

Flavell, G. F. 1987. *The Log of the Panthon.* N. B. Carmony and D. E. Brown, eds. Boulder, Co.: Pruett Publishing Co.

Gale, D. C. 1922. *Proctor: The Story of a Mining Town.* Brattleboro: Vermont Printing Co.

Goldman, E. A. 1937. "A New Mountain Sheep from Lower California." *Proc. Biol. Soc. Washington* 50:29–32.

Grant, M. 1925. "The Establishment of Mt. McKinley National Park."
In *Hunting and Conservation*, G. B. Grinnell and C. Sheldon, eds.
New Haven: Boone and Crockett Club and Yale University Press.
Pp. 438–45.

Griggs, J. 1907. *The Mines of Chihuahua*. A. Vincente Guerrero. N.p.

Grinnell, G. B. 1925. "The National Recreation Conference." In *Hunting and Conservation*, G. B. Grinnell and C. Sheldon, eds. New
Haven: Boone and Crockett Club and Yale University Press. Pp:
471–91.

_____. n.d. "Charles Sheldon." Unpubl. ms. Courtesy of Eleanor
Sheldon Lunde.

Grinnell, G. B., and C. Sheldon, eds. 1925. *Hunting and Conservation*.
New Haven: Boone and Crockett Club and Yale University Press.

Halloran, A. 1950. "Arizona Bighorn Inventory." *Arizona Wildlife
Sportsman*. March:11, 18.

Hartmann. W. K. 1989. *Desert Heart*. Tucson: Fisher Books.

Haslem, L. S., ed. 1922. *Thirty-Year Record, Class of 1890, Yale College*.
New Haven: Yale University Press.

Hernandez-Alvidrez, R., and J. Campoy-Favela. 1989. "Observaciones
Recientes de la Poblacion de Borrego Cimarron en Isla Tiburon,
Sonora, Mexico." *Ecologica* 1(1): 15–22.

Hoffmeister, D. F. 1971. *Mammals of the Grand Canyon*. Urbana: University of Illinois Press.

_____. 1986. *Mammals of Arizona*. Tucson: Arizona Game and Fish
Dept. and University of Arizona Press.

Hornaday, W. T. 1908. *Camp-fires on Desert and Lava*. New York:
Charles Scribner's Sons.

_____. 1924. "Saving the Big Game of Mexico." *Nature Mag.*
October:213–20.

_____. 1931. *Thirty Years War for Wildlife: Gains and Losses in the
Thankless Task*. New York: Charles Scribner's Sons.

Hughes, J. D. 1978. *In the House of Stone and Light: A Human History of
the Grand Canyon*. Grand Canyon, Ariz.: Grand Canyon Nat.
Hist. Assoc.

Ives, R. L. 1955. "Vegetative Changes at Pinacate, Sonora, Mexico."
Science 122(3182): 1235.

_____. 1989. *Land of Lava, Ash, and Sand*. J. W. Byrkit and K. J.
Dahood, eds. Tucson: Arizona Historical Society.

Kaughpy, E. 1946. "Bighorn Sheep of Yuma County." *Arizona Wildlife and Sportsman.* January:1, 4.

Krausman, P. R., J. R. Morgart, and M. Chilelli. 1984. *Annotated Bibliography of Desert Bighorn Sheep Literature, 1897–1983.* Phoenix: Southwest Nat. Hist. Assoc.

Lee, R. M., ed. 1989. *The Desert Bighorn Sheep in Arizona.* Phoenix: Arizona Game and Fish Dept.

Leopold, A. S. 1959. *Wildlife of Mexico.* Berkeley: University of California Press.

Lumholtz, C. 1912. *New Trails in Mexico.* New York: Charles Scribner's Sons.

MacDougal, D. T. 1908. "Across Papagueria." *Plant World.* 11(May): 93–99.

McGee, E. R. 1915. *Life of W J McGee.* Farley, Iowa. Privately printed.

McGee, W. J. 1898. "The Seri Indians." *Annual report of the Bur. of Amer. Ethnol.,* Part 1. 17:1–344.

_____. 1901. "The Old Yuma Trail." *Nat. Geog.* 12(March–April):103–7, 129–43.

_____. 1910. "Notes on the Passenger Pigeon." *Science* 32(835):958–64.

Mearns, E. A. 1907. "Mammals of the Mexican Boundary of the United States." *Bull. U.S. Nat. Mus.* 56:1–530.

Merriam, C. H. 1890. "Results of a Biological Survey of the San Francisco Mountain Region and Desert of the Little Colorado River, Arizona." *N. Amer. Fauna* 3:1–136.

_____. 1897. "*Ovis nelsoni,* a New Mountain Sheep from the Desert Region of Southern California." *Proc. Biol. Soc. Washington* 11:217–18.

_____. 1901. "Two New Bighorns and a New Antelope from Mexico and the United States." *Proc. Biol. Soc. Washington* 14:29–32.

_____. 1916. "*Ovis sheldoni,* a New Mountain Sheep from Sierra del Rosario, Sonora, Mexico." *Proc. Biol. Soc. Washington.* 29: 129–32.

_____. 1930. "Charles Sheldon." Privately reprinted introduction to *The Wilderness of Denali* by C. Sheldon. New York: Charles Scribner's Sons.

Monson, G., and A. R. Phillips. 1981. *Annotated checklist of the Birds of Arizona.* Tucson: University of Arizona Press.

Monson, G., and L. Sumner, eds. 1980. *The Desert Bighorn: Its Life History, Ecology, and Management.* Tucson: University of Arizona Pres.

Moore, T. 1981. *Mt. McKinley: The Pioneer Climbs.* 2nd. ed. Seattle: Mountaineers.

Nabhan, G. P., ed. 1993. *Counting Sheep.* Tucson: University of Arizona Press.

Nelson, E. W. 1884. "A New Geographical Race of the Mountain Sheep (*Ovis montana dalli*, var. nov.) from Alaska." *Proceed. U.S. Nat. Mus.* 7:12–13.

———. 1925. "Status of the Pronghorned Antelope, 1922–1924." *U.S. Dept. Agric. Bull.* No. 1346:1–64.

———. 1928. "Charles Sheldon." *Amer. Forests and Forest Life* 34(November): 659–60.

Nichol, A. A. 1937. "Desert bighorn sheep." *Arizona Wildlife* July:9–16.

———. 1938. "Desert bighorn sheep." *Arizona Wildlife* August:3, 12.

O'Connor, J. 1939. *Game in the Desert.* New York: Derrydale Press.

———. 1961. *The Big Game Animals of North America.* New York: *Outdoor Life* and E. P. Dutton and Co.

———. 1963. *Jack O'Connor's Big Game Hunts.* New York: *Outdoor Life* and E. P. Dutton and Co.

———. 1974. *Sheep and Sheep Hunting.* New York: Winchester Press.

Ortiz, A., ed. 1983. *Handbook of North American Indians*, vol. 10, Southwest. Washington, D.C.: Smithsonian Inst.

Phillips, J. C. 1930. *American Game Mammals and Birds: A Catalogue of Books, 1582 to 1925.* Boston and New York: Boone and Crockett Club and Houghton Mifflin Co.

Reiger, J. F. 1986. *American Sportsmen and the Origins of Conservation.* Revised ed. Norman: University of Oklahoma Press.

Rhode, E. 1988. "Denali Country." *Alaska Geogr.* 15(3): 7–21.

Roosevelt, K. 1912. "The Sheep of the Desert." Reprinted in *Mexican Game Trails*, 1991, N. B. Carmony and D. E. Brown, eds. Norman: University of Oklahoma Press. Pp. 77–92.

Roosevelt, T. 1911. "The American Hunter-Naturalist." *The Outlook.* December 9:854–56.

Ruíz, R. E. 1980. *The Great Rebellion, Mexico, 1905–1924.* W. W. Norton and Co., New York and London.

Russo, J. P. 1956. *The Desert Bighorn Sheep in Arizona: A Research and Management Study.* Phoenix: Arizona Game and Fish Dept.

Sanford, L. C. 1929. "Charles Sheldon." Unpubl. ms. Courtesy of Eleanor Sheldon Lunde.

Schmidt, J. L., and D. L. Gilbert, eds. 1978. *Big Game of North America: Ecology and Management.* Harrisburg, Pa.: Stackpole Books.

Selous, F. C. 1907. *Recent Hunting Trips in British North America.* London: Witherby and Co., and New York: Charles Scribner's Sons.

Shankland, R. 1954. *Steve Mather of the National Parks.* 2nd ed. New York: Alfred A. Knopf.

Sheldon, C. (Carolyn). 1936. "The Mammals of Lake Kedgemakooge and Vicinity, Nova Scotia." *J. Mammal.* 17:207–15.

Sheldon, C. (Charles). 1908. "The Cook Inlet Aborigines." Appendix C, pp. 269–78 in: *To the Top of the Continent,* F. A. Cook. New York: Doubleday, Page and Co.

———. 1909. "List of Birds Observed on the Upper Toklat River, Alaska, 1907–1908." *Auk* 26:66–70.

———. 1911. *The Wilderness of the Upper Yukon.* New York: Charles Scribner's Sons.

———. 1912. *The Wilderness of the North Pacific Coast Islands.* New York: Charles Scribner's Sons.

———. 1912. "Hunting the Big Bear on Montague Island." *Scribner's Magazine.* 51:641–55.

———. 1921. "A Fox Associating with Mountain Sheep on the Kenai Peninsula, Alaska." *J. Mammal.* 2:234.

———. 1923. "The Unprovoked Attack by a 'Brown' Bear." *J. Mammal.* 4:51–52.

———. 1925. "The big game of Chihuahua, Mexico, 1898–1902." In: *Hunting and Conservation,* G. B. Grinnell and C. Sheldon, eds. New Haven: Boone and Crockett Club and Yale University Press. Pp. 138–81.

———. 1925. "The Case of Our Migratory Wild Fowl." Report of the standing committee on wild life, National Conference on Outdoor Recreation *Amer. Forests and Forest Life.* July:416–22.

———. 1927. "The Conservation of the Elk of Jackson Hole, Wyoming." A report by the commission on the conservation of the Jackson Hole elk. National Conference on Outdoor Recreation, Washington, D.C.

———. 1930. *The Wilderness of Denali*. New York: Charles Scribner's Sons.

———. 1979. *The Wilderness of Desert Bighorns and Seri Indians*. D. E. Brown, P. M. Webb, and N. B. Carmony, eds. Phoenix: Arizona Desert Bighorn Sheep Soc.

Sheldon, W. G. 1967. *The Book of the American Woodcock*. Amherst: University of Massachusetts Press.

———. 1975. *The Wilderness Home of the Giant Panda*. Amherst: University of Massachusetts Press.

———. 1981. *Exploring for Wild Sheep in British Columbia in 1931 and 1932*. Clinton, New Jersey: Amwell Press.

Sherwood, M. B. 1965. *The Exploration of Alaska, 1865-1900*. New Haven: Yale University Press.

Shreve, F., and I. L. Wiggins. 1964. *Vegetation and Flora of the Sonoran Desert*. 2 vols. Palo Alto, Calif.: Stanford University Press.

Smith, H. P., and W. S. Rann, eds. 1886. *History of Rutland County, Vermont*. Syracuse, N. Y.: D. Mason and Co.

Stuck, H. 1977. *The Ascent of Denali* (first publ. in 1914). Seattle: The Mountaineers.

Swan, M. G., and D. P. Swan, compilers. 1990. *Early Families of Rutland, Vermont*. Rutland, Vt: Rutland Hist. Soc.

Tinker, B. 1978. *Mexican Wilderness and Wildlife*. Austin: University of Texas Press.

Trefethen, J. B. 1961. *Crusade for Wildlife: Highlights in Conservation Progress*. Harrisburg, Pa.: Boone and Crockett Club and Stackpole Co.

Van Rossem, A. J. 1945. "A Distributional Survey of the Birds of Sonora, Mexico." *Louisiana State Univ. Occas. Pap. Mus. Zool.* 21:1-379.

Wampler, J. 1969. *New Rails to Old Towns: The Region and Story of the Ferrocarriles Chihihuahua al Pacifico*. Berkeley, Calif.: Joseph Wampler.

Wasserman, M. 1975. "Oligarchy and Foreign Enterprise in Porfirian Chihuahua, Mexico, 1876-1911." Ph.D. dissertation, University of Chicago.

———. 1984. *Capitalists, Caciques, and Revolution: The Native Elite and Foreign Enterprise in Chihuahua, Mexico, 1854-1911*. Chapel Hill: University of North Carolina Press.

Welles, R. E., and F. B. Welles. 1961. "The Bighorn of Death Valley." *Fauna of the National Parks of the U.S.*, Fauna Series 6:1-242.

Wild, P. 1979. *Pioneer Conservationists of Western America.* Missoula, Mont.: Mountain Press.

―――. 1985. *Pioneer Conservationists of Eastern America.* Missoula, Mont.: Mountain Press.

Index

About the editors

NEIL B. CARMONY, formerly a chemist with the U.S. Geological Survey, has coedited several books about naturalists and adventurers.

DAVID E. BROWN is a Phoenix-based journalist and consulting biologist with twenty-five years' experience with the Arizona Game and Fish Department.